WILLIAMS-SONOMA

ROME

AUTHENTIC RECIPES CELEBRATING THE FOODS OF THE WORLD

Recipes and Text
MAUREEN B. FANT

Photographs
JEAN-BLAISE HALL

General Editor
CHUCK WILLIAMS

Oxmoor House®

CONTENTS

RECIPES

ANTIPASTI

PRIMI

SECONDI

CONTORNI

DOLCI

INTRODUCTION

The best Roman food tastes like what it is. Artichokes taste like artichokes, lamb like lamb. Herbs are freshly cut and are usually limited to just one variety per dish. Sometimes the eloquence of this simplicity is lost on visitors, but *la cucina romana* rewards those who take the time to get to know it.

CULINARY HISTORY

The arrival of the tomato and potato from the New World in the sixteenth century did not have a dramatic effect on the Roman diet, despite the wonderful things that local cooks would learn to do with them. Centuries ago, as today, the core of the Roman menu was olives and olive oil, legumes, cured pork, lamb, organ meats, garden-fresh vegetables and wild greens, sheep's milk cheeses and other dairy products, chewy bread baked in wood-burning ovens, pasta, fresh fish, and salted anchovies. Drinks have been equally consistent, with local wine and spring water accompanying meals.

At the start of the first millennium BC, Rome, today the focal point of the Lazio (Latium) region, was little more than a river, some uninhabited hills, and a handful of shepherds' huts. Within less than a thousand years, there was a thriving city, a culture, sophisticated systems of transportation and communications, and domination of the Western world. Bread in the capital was baked with grain from North Africa, and dates came from Syria. The food distribution was analogous to that of Victorian and Edwardian England or the contemporary global trade network. But even during the height of the Roman Empire, there were always statesmen and writers to lament the good old days when a bowl of warm spelt was all the luxury a good Roman needed. Some of the complaining took the form of satirical or hyperbolic accounts of contemporary excess, often with a political agenda. Petronius's first-century AD fictional account of the newly rich Trimalchio's vulgar and extravagant banquet ensured that future generations would think of Roman food as based on a diet of larks' tongues and dormice.

With the fall of the empire, Rome entered a period of isolation and underpopulation. Roman popular cooking from the sixth to the nineteenth century can be viewed nearly as a whole. The elaborate water distribution system of the ancients was out of commission from the sixth century to the papacy of Nicholas V (1447–55), and the population shrank significantly, with fewer than fifty thousand souls rattling around within walls built for a city of one million. During the Middle Ages, residents huddled near the Tiber, the principal source of water. They occupied and sometimes destroyed the ancient monuments, and created the architectural imprint that the heart of old Rome still bears today.

The face of Rome changed dramatically after it became the capital of the Kingdom of Italy in 1870, not least because of a sharp increase in population. But until then gardens within the walls, irrigated by canals and streams, provided city dwellers with celery, artichokes, cabbages, chard, and other vegetables. Until the nineteenth century, mills floated on the Tiber and used the river's hydraulic power to grind flour for bread and homemade pasta. Egg pasta was for the rich; the poor made their dough with only flour and water. The usual sauce was often a mixture of pork fat and pecorino until the tomato gained culinary acceptance in the eighteenth century. Dried industrial pasta did not arrive until the late nineteenth century.

Romans went outside the walls to pick the wild chicories and lettuces that covered the countryside. Porcini and *ovoli,* mushrooms

that nowadays command high prices, grew plentifully and were an important part of the popular kitchen.

The city's earliest restaurants were the ancestors of today's wine bar and *tavola calda* (literally, "hot table," a place to get a cheap, hot meal). Examples of the *thermopolium* (hot shop) preserved in Pompeii and in the ancient port, Ostia Antica, show how earthenware jars were embedded in the shop's counter, while wall paintings show the menu of onions, olives, and cheese.

Although for much of its history Rome drew visitors from all parts of the known world, mass tourism began with the medieval Christian pilgrimages, particularly the jubilee year of 1300. For centuries, pilgrims ate at taverns and *osterie*, all of which had names that could be easily depicted in symbols for illiterate patrons (The Falcon, The Two Swords, and so on). Each served a specialty, such as pot roast or slow-cooked pork, and carafes of wine, some of it from vineyards within the city walls. Northern Europeans

on the Grand Tour in the eighteenth and nine-teenth centuries enjoyed picturesque *osterie* that were not unlike their predecessors.

The economic boom that followed World War II brought changes both in demography and at the table. While American tourists threw their coins in the Trevi Fountain and American movie stars went to work at Cinecittà (dubbed Hollywood-on-the-Tiber), workers from southern Italy introduced new regional culinary influences, such as pizza, to the capital.

In those days, affluence continued to mean calories, of which Ristorante Alfredo's signature *fettuccine al triplo burro* (fettuccine with triple butter, more commonly known as fettuccine Alfredo, and still going strong), can stand as emblematic. Cream sauces trickled down to the trattoria menu as well and weren't uprooted until the days of the post-1968 countercultural eateries, the so-called alternative restaurants. They specialized in dishes that rebelled against tradition, such as salads with canned corn, whose main

virtues were probably ease of preparation and a total departure from Roman tradition. Fortunately, all the while, a decent *spaghetti alla carbonara* could still be found at any number of neighborhood trattorias.

By the late 1980s, talented chefs with professional training began using the finest ingredients available to offer original dishes to a more sophisticated clientele. *Cucina creativa,* Italy's answer to nouvelle cuisine, established itself in Rome in a handful of very good, very expensive restaurants. Meanwhile, in a somewhat related movement, traditional Roman food (and regional food in general) was being rediscovered and lightened up. After the opening of Rome's first McDonald's in the Piazza di Spagna in 1985, traditionalists went on the warpath. Soon, the old-school dishes like *pasta alla gricia,* almost forgotten, became the foodies' shibboleth. Around this time the Slow Food Association, based in Piedmont, and the influential *Gambero Rosso* magazine began to raise the profile of both traditional and innovative cooking.

CONTEMPORARY CUISINE

Located almost in the geographic center of Italy, and for millennia a magnet for pilgrims and visitors, Rome might well have become the gastronomic world in microcosm. Although restaurants that feature creative dishes or imported ingredients are on the rise, Roman menus remain surprisingly loyal to local tradition.

There may be a cell phone on the table, but the main influence on Roman eating is still tradition. Indeed, it sometimes seems that the newer the restaurant, the older the menu, with chefs now doing historical research and chatting with their grandmothers when it comes time to develop recipes.

Cooking in Rome remains ingredient driven, and choices are strictly seasonal. Pasta is the pillar of the cuisine, surrounded by extraordinary vegetables and good, simply cooked meat and fish. Most dishes have only a few elements and fewer secrets: if it is there, you can usually taste it and identify it. Innovation can mean adding one additional ingredient to *spaghetti alla carbonara.*

Not that all Romans eat in a museum, however. Some brilliant and creative chefs are pushing the boundaries. It's just that most people like what they've always eaten, and with good reason. They like looking forward to fava (broad) beans in May, figs in June, peaches in July, and persimmons in October. Bankers and bus drivers alike are happy on Thursday mornings because they know their favorite trattoria will be serving gnocchi for lunch. On Tuesdays and Fridays, it's fish. At Christmas and Easter, Romans still give one another gifts of home-baked cookies. How long modern life (complete with encroaching supermarkets and shrinking lunch hours) will allow the status quo to survive is of great concern to many.

Although not immune to food fashion or fad, in general Rome is blissfully free of the sort of fanaticism that eliminates entire food groups from the diet. If you discount six espressos a day and a weakness for pastry and deep-frying—and salami and pancetta—the Roman diet fits the Mediterranean ideal: plenty of fruits and vegetables, lots of legumes, fresh fish, and small amounts of meat, little of it red. The main fat used is olive oil. Delicate Roman gelato makes favorite brands outside Italy seem too dense and rich in comparison. Wine is preferred to hard liquor, and the tap water is excellent.

Few vegetarian restaurants exist: if you can have a *carciofo alla romana* (page 159) for your main course in an ordinary trattoria, what's the point? However, shops that offer *biologico* (organic) food are thriving, and even macrobiotic eating has its fans. Dishes that began to enter the Roman consciousness through the vegetarian-organic back door in the 1990s, such as hummus and tabbouleh, are standards among young people and at the occasional casual party.

Some outside influences maintain a culinary presence in Rome, of which the most venerable are dishes from other regions of Italy. Even a restaurant in Rome that serves *ribollita,* the vegetable soup on every Florentine menu, or *seadas,* the classic Sardinian honey-drenched, cheese-filled fried pastry, is considered exotic.

You'll find almost no French restaurants in Rome, but you may come across a thriving *birreria* (beer hall) offering frankfurters, sausages, *crauti* (sauerkraut), and, of course, an array of beer. Truly foreign restaurants used to be isolated phenomena. For years, a lone Hungarian restaurant stood alongside the Forum of Trajan, but it became Chinese, and several owners later is now Sicilian, a favorite gastronomic ethnicity (a much more labor-intensive and richly textured cuisine than the Roman). Yet no more than a few Sicilian restaurants are found in the capital.

There are certainly more Indian eateries than in the past, and Chinese restaurants have proliferated, but unfortunately much of the food served in them is frozen or canned. Most of the few Eritrean and Middle Eastern spots mainly attract new foreign residents and the occasional curious Roman seeking a change of pace from familiar regional fare.

The concept of fusion cooking has not really arrived in Rome. Most mixing is limited to the combining of regional specialties.

Well-thought-out departures from tradition are instead called *cucina creativa*. A chef like Heinz Beck of La Pergola (Rome's only Michelin two-star restaurant), at the Cavalieri Hilton Hotel atop Monte Mario, or Angelo Troiani of Il Convivio, near Piazza Navona, may let their formidable fantasies run freely— they may even use foreign ingredients—but if you read the whole of any given menu, you'll know what time of year it is, where you are, and that the menu was not composed by a committee. Beck's signature is a multiplicity of little dishes, such as artichokes five ways. Troiani is well known for his instinct for combination: imagine sweet shrimp (prawns) with a touch of bitter Campari.

A trip through the aisles of a Roman supermarket reveals a world of canned sauces and frozen pasta that will quickly dash the illusions of any visitor who imagines happy Italian families tucking into mamma's cooking every day and twice on Sunday. The fact is that some modern Italians are embracing convenience in the form of canned, frozen,

and packaged foods. But even harried parents who gratefully accept a time- or energy-saving innovation anywhere they find it, or a single person who takes home a hearty spit-roasted chicken from the corner *rosticceria* rather than face the kitchen in solitude, usually know how to cook a decent meal in a pinch. The advice of a mother, an uncle, or a friend is, after all, only a phone call away.

Many people do, of course, love to cook and will gladly spend hours preparing a special dinner for friends, turning out everything from scratch. That is the moment to share one's discoveries and gastronomic treasures: the best *mozzarella di bufala* in the capital, a single-vineyard Amarone wine that has been saved for the right natural Gorgonzola, or a spit-roasted leg of lamb from Abruzzo, just big enough for four. Indeed, some of the best food in Rome can be found in modest home kitchens, where Romans make simple but flavorful meals using many of the same local ingredients their ancestors did in centuries past.

DINING OUT

Rome boasts its share of exclusive Michelin star restaurants, but the eatery par excellence is the trattoria, the casual neighborhood restaurant serving simple, traditional local food. It used to be the place to go for food just like you ate at home. Today, a trattoria is the place to find hearty and authentic regional dishes.

The small, family-run restaurant, whether serving spaghetti or creative delicacies, provides the most satisfying dining experiences in Rome. The best-loved places tend to be small, and the owner is on-site, in either the dining room or the kitchen. And though many people try all the new spots in their search for gastronomic thrills, most return again and again to a couple of favorite establishments in their own neighborhood.

When Romans go out to eat, the main appeal may not be the food, but rather the chance to *stare insieme*—to be together with their friends, with someone else doing the work. They'll often order the foods they know, especially those that are too difficult or time-consuming to make at home. There remains a strongly traditional current in Roman dining habits and restaurant menus, with the same dishes continually reappearing. But only lazy cooks make a boring meal—even Sophocles, Euripides, and Shakespeare retold old stories, making them richer and more interesting along the way. As awareness of wines, top ingredients, and gourmet foods from around Italy continues to grow, even some stalwart trattoria menus have become more interesting and sophisticated.

Hallmarks of the Roman Table

The day starts early with a coffee and pastry at *il bar*. In Rome, the bar is a coffee stop and gathering place—not just a place to drink alcohol. The next trip to the bar, for a break or quick lunch, could involve a *tramezzino, pizzetta,* or *medaglione*—each one a different kind of snack or sandwich. At lunch or dinner, restaurants and trattorias offer unhurried meals of two to four courses. A long dinner with plenty of wine and talk is typically the night's entertainment. Many wine bars (page 54) offer meals that tend to be lighter than those from traditional eateries and are a good choice in the evening, especially if you've had a large lunch.

Romans are not in general known for their polished manners, and waiters are often gruff or brusque. The lack of attention to service puts some foreign visitors off, but they should not take it personally—it's just the local way. What the waiters lack in charm, they usually make up for in skill. And if there were no other reason to learn some Italian, it would be worth it to be able to question your waiter about the menu, what the table next to you is having, the size of the clams, and what bottle of wine would go well with your meal.

Attention to décor has come late to the Roman restaurant scene and is not an effective indicator of price and quality. Some of the finest eateries are at best nondescript: what passes for décor might be a homely accretion of framed pictures and other memorabilia. Some restaurants, however, are particularly known for their good looks. At La Terrazza, in the Hotel Eden, near Via Veneto, picture

windows mean the beautiful view of Rome's rooftops outshines the rest of the room. In the summer, La Pergola sets their tables on the terrace to exploit its extraordinary panorama; in winter the dining room, with plenty of polished wood and brass, and fresh flowers, is no less welcoming. Likewise, restaurant Vecchia Roma's ornate rooms are used most often in winter. In summer, the picturesque Piazza Campitelli, where Vecchia Roma is located, provides possibly the most charming ambience in town. Studied minimalism, as at the 'Gusto wine bar and restaurant, is making inroads in baroque Rome.

Standard-Setting Restaurants

Some of the top restaurants in Rome continue a tradition that has lasted through generations, and in some cases, centuries. When the French essayist Montaigne visited Rome in 1580, he stopped at a combination inn and tavern between the Tiber and Piazza Navona called L'Orso (The Bear). And when the celebrated Milanese chef-restaurateur

Gualtiero Marchesi opened his elegant outpost in the capital in 2001 in the same location, he kept the name Hostaria dell'Orso (Inn of the Bear). The venerable Ristorante La Campana, not far away on a street of the same name, has been there since at least the early 1500s. The Hostaria dell'Orso has a piano bar and serves a highly refined creative and classic menu. La Campana is beloved for its trattoria-style *spaghetti all'amatriciana, carciofi alla romana,* and other Roman staples.

Downriver in Testaccio, at Checchino dal 1887, the Mariani siblings serve affluent diners the *quinto quarto* dishes (page 143) that their great-grandmother made for the slaughterhouse workers from across the street in the nineteenth century. At Al Presidente, a few steps from the Trevi Fountain, Sebastiano Allegrini serves raw-fish "Mediterranean sushi" and a number of traditional fish and meat dishes in the same space his parents once ran a trattoria. Creative chef Agata Parisella, with her husband, Romeo Caraccio, transformed her family's trattoria into the

elegant Ristorante Agata e Romeo, near the church of Santa Maria Maggiore. Massimo Riccioli turned his father's place near the Pantheon, on Via della Rosetta, into the top seafood restaurant in Rome, La Rosetta.

The neighborhood restaurants of Rome, collectively and loosely grouped under the term "trattoria," cover a very broad range of cuisines and degrees of elegance. Lucia and Augusto, two trattorias in Trastevere, represent the old style—with simple rooms and simpler menus. The *primi* offerings will usually include *pasta alla carbonara* and/or *amatriciana,* while *secondi* usually include simple grilled meats. Such places are often frequented by tourists seeking the real Rome and Romans seeking a sure thing at a good price. Enoteca Corsi, on Via del Gesù, evolved from the back room of a wine shop. La Piazzetta, near Via Cavour, boasts an updated menu and great desserts. Colline Emiliane, near Piazza Barberini, and La Gensola, in Trastevere, offering Emilian and Sicilian dishes, respectively, are among the few regional trattorias.

MARKETS

The large municipal markets and the small, specialized food shops surrounding them are quite simply the best places to buy groceries—and to get a recipe, catch up on neighborhood gossip, have a lesson on the correct use of six kinds of tomatoes, and learn the right way to cut *puntarelle* and *carciofi*.

Shopping for food in Rome's local markets is a skill that foreign residents and visitors would be wise to learn quickly and well. You need to know how to insist on the best quality and how to assert your place in "line." It is assumed that if you are not jostling, you are just looking. Visitors with no local kitchens in which to cook their purchases need not miss the experience. Armed with just a few key words, they can acquire an excellent picnic to enjoy in one of the city's many parks.

In Rome, you don't make a shopping list. You begin to plan your meal when you see what looks best at the market. Depending on the season, you'll find fresh fava (broad) beans and peas already shelled, *puntarelle* (Catalonian chicory) skillfully cut, Borettana onions (small, round, and flat) peeled and ready to cook *in agrodolce,* and all the leafy greens—spinach, broccoli rabe, and various chicories—divested of their tough stems.

Every quarter of Rome has one large and a number of small markets, most of them open six mornings a week, Monday through Saturday. The most famous central markets are those in Piazza Testaccio and Piazza Campo de' Fiori, and the one near Piazza Vittorio Emanuele. Tucked here and there are miniature versions serving residents of the immediate neighborhood. Look for one close to the Trevi Fountain in front of the restaurant Al Presidente, on Via Bocca de Leone, near the Piazza di Spagna, and the charming market near the church of San Saba, in the Aventino area.

Not much difference exists between a market stall and a standard small grocery shop except for the hours (the shop reopens in the afternoon) and the presence of walls. The most colorful shops are single purpose but broadly interpreted. The *salumeria* or *salsamenteria* sells prosciutto, salamis, and cheeses. The *fruttivendolo* is a greengrocer. The *pescheria* sells fish, and the *macelleria* sells meat. An *alimentari* is a general-purpose food shop that does not carry produce.

Campo de' Fiori

The open-air stalls in Campo de' Fiori form the main market of the Centro Storico. Its oft-photographed array of flowers for sale seems to console the imposing central statue of Giordano Bruno, the philosopher-monk burned at the stake here in 1600. The large, rectangular piazza is located between the beautiful Piazza Farnese, where the French Embassy occupies a magnificent Renaissance palazzo (Palazzo Farnese), and the small piazza that contains the Palazzo della Cancelleria. Around the three piazzas, and along the narrow streets that surround them, are many popular trattorias, bars, and miscellaneous eateries aimed at tourists and young people, as well as actual residents of this once working-class neighborhood, now a coveted address.

It's not the fault of the vendors, who are as real as any you'll find in the city, but rather of geography that Campo de' Fiori is the market that draws the most tourists. If you can manage the crowds, you'll find the quality and variety of the produce here are first-rate. Look for the large stall of Claudio Zampa in the middle of the piazza. He sells a wide range of the best seasonal produce and even some exotic fruits. A few fish stalls grouped in one corner sell excellent sea bass, fresh anchovies, and other local favorites.

At another corner of the piazza, close to Piazza Farnese, is one of the best-loved bakeries in all of Rome, Antico Forno del Campo de' Fiori. Sample the *pizza bianca* (page 48), plain, or filled with any number of toppings. They also bake a fine *torta di mele* (apple cake), a little-known Roman tradition.

Piazza Vittorio

One of the only places in Rome where you begin to wonder if you're still in Italy is the labyrinthine indoor market between Via Filippo Turati and Via Lamarmora, just south of the Termini station. This is the Esquilino neighborhood, named for one of Rome's canonical seven hills, and for the past few decades, this is where Rome's growing population of immigrants from Africa, Asia, and the Middle East has come to settle. In the spacious sky-lit market of Piazza Vittorio, you'll have no trouble buying halal meat, green beans from Morocco, dried fish from Bangladesh, and every kind of spice, rice, and legume. In addition you'll find every sort of local fruit and vegetable, as well as fresh Mediterranean fish and plenty of fresh meats to choose from.

Piazza Testaccio

The heart of the food-oriented Testaccio quarter is the big square market—roofed but open—of Piazza Testaccio. Nearly a whole side of the square is devoted to fish sellers, such as Rosa and Nello, first in the line, who will fillet your fresh anchovies or skin your moray eel while you buy your fruit. Near the fish stalls is the tomato man: here you'll find the finest array of tomatoes in the market, from fleshy Ligurian Cuore di Bue tomatoes to tiny Sicilian Datteri, roughly the size and shape of dates. On the far side of the market are the vendors who grow or gather their own produce (the others buy from the wholesale markets). Check here for wild chicory or for the freshest carrots. The customers are fairly well heeled, but the atmosphere is genuine: there is plenty of good-natured yelling, chatter, and ribbing among the vendors, who can trim artichokes, *puntarelle,* and *broccoletti* like no one else in the city.

Meat is still an important fixture in this neighborhood, where the old slaughterhouse was located and all its workers lived and ate. Meats of all kinds are well represented in the market and shops around the square. Gourmets from all over come to this area just to visit the nearby Volpetti shop on Via Marmorata. Here you will find a store jam-packed with the finest cured meats, fresh and aged cheeses, and condiments from every corner of Italy and beyond.

FLAVORS OF THE NEIGHBORHOODS

If every neighborhood in Rome is well supplied with restaurants, trattorias, *gelaterie,* and coffee bars, as well as places to buy superb greens, *mozzarella di bufala,* and *prosciutto di Parma,* what makes them all so different? It must be the history.

In the first century AD, as part of his plan for remaking the city of Rome, the emperor Augustus divided it into fourteen districts. Today, after two millennia, the city is still made up of districts, or *rioni,* which now number twenty-two within the city's walls (outside are quarters, suburbs, and zones). Many *rioni* preserve a particular urban personality, a combination of the history, architecture, monuments, amenities, and, of course, residents of the area. And though neighborhood stores provide all the essentials for those living nearby, the finest local shops and eateries entice people from around the city and around the world.

Trastevere

The name Trastevere means "across the Tiber," and refers to the area on the west bank, south of the river's bend, opposite the Campo Marzio and Testaccio. The *trasteverini* like to call themselves the last true Romans, and they celebrate their identity each summer with the Festa de' Noantri ("the rest of us," meaning the *trasteverini* themselves), held in July. But the densely populated Trastevere district, Rione XIII, is also overflowing with artists, foreign residents, and visitors from less lively neighborhoods. It is home to the city's only English-language cinema and to one of Rome's oldest churches, beautiful Santa Maria in Trastevere (look for stunning mosaics inside). At night, the areas around Santa Maria and the nearby church of Santa Cecilia, with their small ivy-hung palazzi and narrow,

winding streets, bustle with a kind of postmillennial dolce vita atmosphere. Young people of all stripes and piercings come here to eat, drink, and socialize with each other, which has made living in this once-tranquil area something of a challenge.

Trastevere is arguably Rome's most food-laden neighborhood. Within steps of Piazza San Cosimato, with its open-air market, are shops selling coffee beans and exotic spices, notably Filippetti, on Via Natale del Grande. Tubs of superb ricotta and bread from the wood-fired ovens in the town of Genzano are both for sale at Antica Caciara Trasteverina on Via San Francesco a Ripa, along with the best wines and *salumi.* You'll also find every kind of sandwich, pizza, and *dolce.* This is also the area to come to meet friends at a hip café.

Amid the exuberance you'll find some very good places for fine, but not fancy, dining. Ristorante Paris, on the small Piazza San Calisto, between Piazza San Cosimato and Piazza di Santa Maria in Trastevere, features both Jewish and traditional Roman *quinto quarto* dishes (page 143), as well as excellent fish. Checco er Carettiere offers traditional, stick-to-the-ribs Roman fare (don't miss the *supplì* and other fried dishes) near Ponte Sisto, the pedestrian bridge. Just above the heart of Trastevere, atop the Gianicolo (Janiculum Hill), opposite the Porta di San Pancrazio, is perhaps the area's most stylish restaurant, L'Antico Arco, known for serving superb cutting-edge cuisine that mixes the traditional with the avant-garde.

Centro Storico

The famous outdoor market in Piazza Campo de' Fiori is the gastronomic heart of one of the most archaeologically interesting areas of Rome's center, covering several small *rioni*. Unlike the Forum area, where the archaeology is strictly delineated, the area extending from the Pantheon and Piazza Navona south to the Tiber and just east to the Theater of Marcellus is itself one big archaeological site, with the ancient remains enclosed and embedded in the fabric of the medieval, Renaissance, and modern city.

Fortunately, you will find plenty to eat as you try—perhaps less successfully—to trace the outlines of the first century BC Theater of Pompey in the curving streets that lie just east of the Campo de' Fiori, or as you contemplate the origins of the granite fountains of Piazza Farnese (the Baths of Caracalla).

In the photogenic, fountain-filled Piazza Navona, itself an ancient racetrack, posh café Tre Scalini serves the famous *tartufo* (ice cream truffle) that it invented. Visit the streets around the Pantheon, Rome's best preserved ancient temple, for excellent gelato (try Fiocco di Neve or the wonderful flavors at Giolitti) and the famous coffee at bars Sant'Eustachio and Tazza d'Oro (page 34). Trattoria Armando, with a menu that changes frequently and superb desserts, and the elegant seafood specialist Ristorante La Rosetta are two outstanding restaurants in the area.

Narrow, pedestrian-only Via dei Giubbonari is home to both the city's best fried salt cod, at the little Filettaro Santa Barbara, and charming Roscioli, a gourmet shop-cum-eatery. From there it's a step across Via Arenula to the Jewish quarter (Rione XI) and the Antico Forno del Ghetto, a hole-in-the-wall kosher bakery known for having the most formidable ricotta cake in town. You don't have to go to the Ghetto for fried artichokes, but lunch at Piperno, on Via Monte de' Cenci, or at nearby Da Giggetto, is a good excuse for a walk along the Via del Portico d'Ottavia, which holds some of the capital's oldest continuously inhabited buildings.

Testaccio

Architecturally, Testaccio, Rione XX, which lies along the Tiber just south of the city center, is relatively new. Most buildings in the area were built during or after an 1873 zoning plan that turned the former river port and open space into a workers' quarter of public housing and industrial plants. The neighborhood takes its name from the nickname of an archaeological site, a large hill of neatly stacked, broken amphorae dating to the fourth century.

It was, however, the *mattatoio,* or slaughterhouse, built between 1888 and 1891, that gave the quarter its modern association with food and eating, thanks to the trattorias that prepared appetizing recipes using *il quinto quarto,* the lesser cuts of meat and innards given to the workers as part of their pay. The structure is still standing, with the allegorical sculpture group that includes a proud ox over its entrance (page 143), and has been put to various uses over the years.

The trattorias are still there, too, though most of them cater to a younger, more fashionable crowd than even ten or twenty years ago. Checchino dal 1887, on Via di Monte Testaccio, has been in business for more than a century, as its name attests, serving guests the finest Piedmontese cheeses after their tripe and *coda alla vaccinara* (oxtail stew). Da Oio a Casa Mia, on Via Galvani; Da Bucatino, on Via Luca della Robbia; and Agustarello, on Via Giovanni Branca, are among the Testaccio trattorias that offer economical versions of the neighborhood classics. Those who want to eat something lighter can have a snack at Volpetti Più, a *tavola calda* offering eat-in versions of many of the prepared foods—such as pizza, *supplì, baccalà alla romana,* stuffed zucchini, and much more—sold at the well-stocked Volpetti shop on Via Marmorata.

Prati

Sometimes it seems as though the people who assigned the street names in Rome had a sense of humor. Thus one of the broad avenues that runs from the Tiber to near the Vatican is named Via Cola di Rienzo, after the fourteenth-century popular leader who tried to wrest temporal rule of Rome from the pope and nobles. This is Prati (literally "meadows"); its gracious grid plan dates to the years after 1870, when Rome had just become capital of the united Italy.

Locals come to the area, and especially Via Cola di Rienzo, for specialty foods to take home or to provide sustenance while they make the rounds of the neighborhood's famous shopping. Some Romans won't eat a spit-roasted chicken unless it comes from Franchi, the combination gourmet shop and *tavola calda* at number 200. Others won't make a pot of coffee without their favorite blend from Castroni, next door at number 196. Prati's covered market is another popular draw thanks to the excellent produce and other foods available there, and also because of its distinctive white 1928 structure. The market is referred to as Piazza dell'Unità, but

the "piazza" is actually a stretch of the same Via Cola di Rienzo. Many Romans swear by the historic Gelateria Pellacchia, at number 103 on the same street, founded in 1904 and still whipping cream by hand.

Monti and Esquilino

The large swath of the city extending roughly from the line between the Colosseum and the Basilica of San Giovanni in Laterano north to the Termini station corresponds approximately to two *rioni,* Monti and Esquilino. Wedged between Via Cavour and Via Nazionale are the narrow streets of Monti, which in antiquity was known as Suburra, a notorious slum. Farther toward Termini are the broad avenues of the Esquilino. There, amid roomy four- and five-story *palazzi* built in the late nineteenth and early twentieth centuries, new immigrants from Asia and Africa are opening up many shops and restaurants.

Gastronomically, the whole area is dominated by the Piazza Vittorio market (page 22). The gourmet apex of the neighborhood is Ristorante Agata e Romeo, on everyone's list of Rome's top eateries. The small, down-to-earth Trattoria Monti, around the corner on Via San Vito, serves plates from the Marche region, northeast of Rome. On Via Merulana, within sight of the Basilica of Santa Maria Maggiore, the breads and sweets of Panella draw customers from all over town, while down in Monti, Pizzeria Leonina (Via Leonina) serves exceptional pizza *al taglio* cut into neat squares on wooden boards. If there is one place that makes the whole neighborhood smile, it's gelateria Fassi, located under the shaded porticoes of once-grand Piazza Vittorio Emanuele. This area is a bit run-down now, and can be dangerous at night due to its proximity to Termini Station. Nonetheless, it is worth making the trek out here for a visit to Fassi, more of an ice-cream parlor than a *gelateria,* and much beloved by locals and visitors alike since 1928.

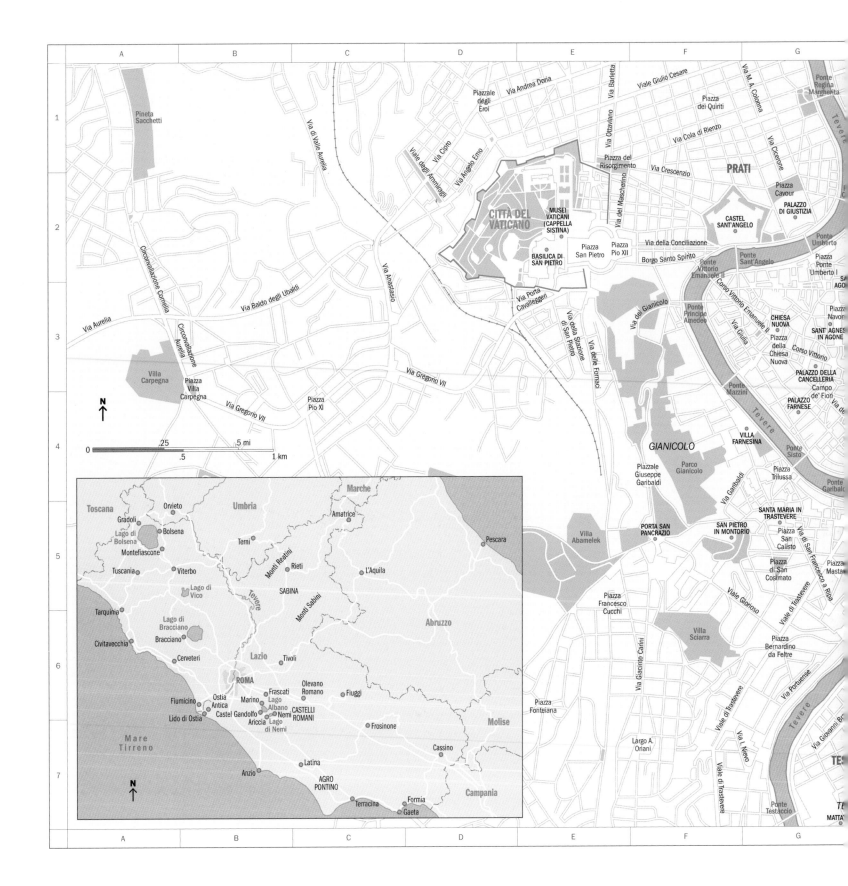

Pineta
Sacchetti

Via di Valle Aurelia

Via degli Ammiragli

Via Angelo Emo

Via Cipro

Piazzale
degli
Eroi

Via Andrea Doria

Via Barletta

Viale Giulio Cesare

Via M. A. Colonna

Via Ottaviano

Piazza
dei Quiriti

Ponte
Regina
Margherita

Via Cola di Rienzo

Via Cicerone

Tevere

Piazza del
Risorgimento

Via Crescenzio

PRATI

Piazza del
Risorgimento

Circonvallazione Cornelia

Via Anastasio

CITTÀ DEL
VATICANO

MUSEI
VATICANI
(CAPPELLA
SISTINA)

Via del Mascherino

Piazza
Cavour

PALAZZO
DI GIUSTIZIA

CASTEL
SANT'ANGELO

Via Baldo degli Ubaldi

Circonvallazione
Aurelia

Via Aurelia

BASILICA DI
SAN PIETRO

Piazza
San Pietro

Piazza
Pio XII

Via della Conciliazione

Borgo Santo Spirito

Ponte
Umberto

Ponte
Sant'Angelo

Piazza
Ponte
Umberto I

SA
AGO

Via Porta
Cavalleggeri

Via della Stazione
di San Pietro

Ponte
Vittorio
Emanuele II

Ponte
Navon

Villa
Carpegna

Piazza
Villa
Carpegna

Via della Fornaci

Via del Gianicolo

Ponte
Principe
Amedeo

Corso Vittorio Emanuele II

Via Giulia

CHIESA
NUOVA

SANT'AGNES
IN AGONE

Piazza
della
Chiesa
Nuova

Corso Vittorio

Via Gregorio VII

Piazza
Villa
Carpegna

Via Gregorio VII

Piazza
Pio XI

PALAZZO DELLA
CANCELLERIA

Ponte
Mazzini

Campo
de' Fiori

PALAZZO
FARNESE

N

0   .25   .5 mi

.5   1 km

GIANICOLO

VILLA
FARNESINA

Ponte
Sisto

Piazza
Trilussa

Ponte
Garibald

Piazzale
Giuseppe
Garibaldi

Parco
Gianicolo

Via Garibaldi

SANTA MARIA IN
TRASTEVERE

Villa
Abamelek

PORTA SAN
PANCRAZIO

SAN PIETRO
IN MONTORIO

Piazza
San
Calisto

Piazza
di San
Cosimato

Piaz
Mast

Via di San Francesco a Ripa

Viale Glorioso

Piazza
Francesco
Cucchi

Villa
Sciarra

Piazza
Bernardino
da Feltre

Via Giacinto Carini

Viale di Trastevere

Piazza
Fonteiana

Via Portuense

Largo A.
Oriani

Tevere

Via Giovanni Br

TE

Viale di Trastevere

Via I. Nievo

Ponte
Testaccio

TI

MATTA

Lazio inset map:

Toscana

Gradoli

Lago di
Bolsena

Bolsena

Orvieto

Umbria

Marche

Montefiascone

Terni

Amatrice

Tuscania

Viterbo

Lago di
Vico

Monti Reatini

Rieti

Pescara

Tarquinia

Tevere

SABINA

L'Aquila

Lago di
Bracciano

Monti Sabini

Abruzzo

Civitavecchia

Bracciano

Cerveteri

Lazio

Tivoli

Fiumicino

ROMA

Frascati

Olevano
Romano

Fiuggi

Ostia
Antica

Marino

Lago
Albano

Molise

Lido di Ostia

Castel Gandolfo

Nemi

CASTELLI
ROMANI

Ariccia

Lago
di Nemi

Frosinone

Mare
Tirreno

Cassino

Latina

Anzio

AGRO
PONTINO

Campania

N

Terracina

Formia

Gaeta

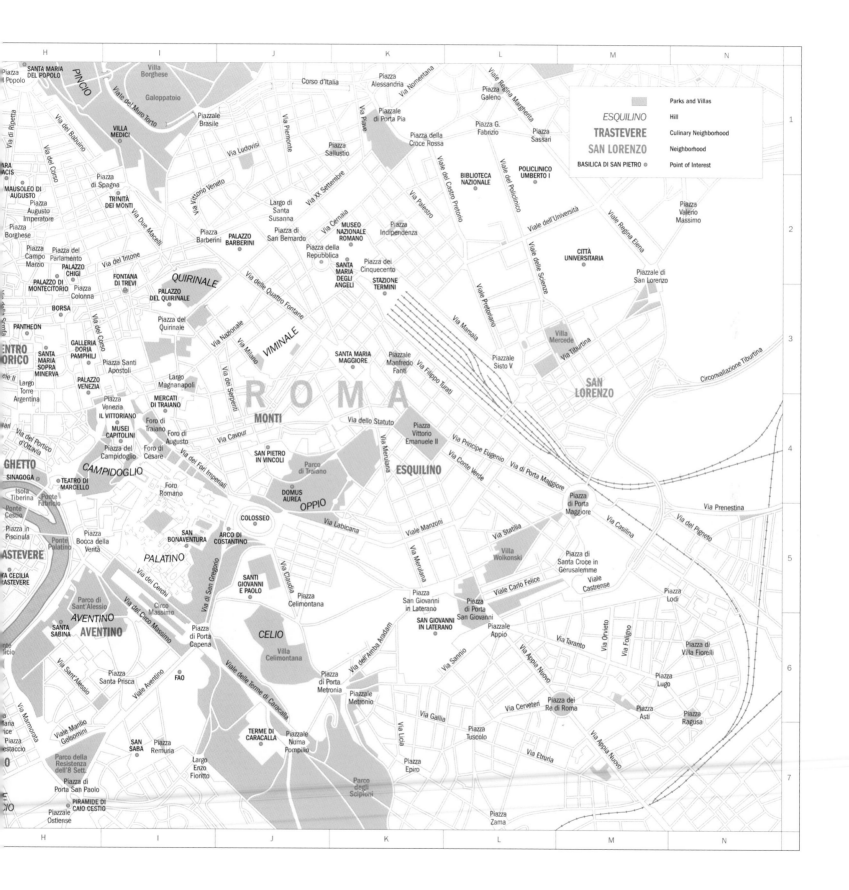

Best of **ROME**

Whether it is served *lungo, ristretto, tiepido, bollente, macchiato, zuccherato,* or *amaro,* coffee in Rome is some of the best in the world. What makes it taste so good? It's not the air, the water, the machines, or even the roast. It's the human factor—the magic touch of an expert *barista.*

COFFEE

Coffee drinking, or at least proximity to it, is inseparable from life in Rome. It's probably not an exaggeration to say that most relationships in Rome begin with an invitation for coffee. Working people may make several trips to the bar every day, and everyone does well to align with a local bar, which can serve as a place to leave a letter, pick up a key, or hear the latest neighborhood news.

When it comes to buying ground beans for home use, Romans are not so much coffee experts (though many are) as coffee partisans. There may be a perfectly good bar right next door, but they'll ride a bus across town to buy a few days' worth at a favorite coffee roaster (invariably also a bar), because nothing else will do. On the return trip, the passengers on the bus will know that another coffee lover is on his or her way home with a bag of fine

powder that was freshly ground from beans roasted nearly black. The importance of a perfect cup of coffee at home is evidenced by the array of sizes of stove-top coffeemakers. Two cups are never made in a four-cup pot, and many people even own a one-cup pot for perfect solo servings.

Don't ask for a latte at a Roman bar unless you want a glass of milk. Coffee with hot milk, usually served at home in an extra-large cup or, at bars, in a glass, is *caffelatte.* When it is in a cup, with milk steamed to produce a head of froth, it is a cappuccino, or *cappuccio* in local vernacular. Both are really considered breakfast drinks, though a cappuccino is acceptable throughout the day. However, only tourists ask for a cappuccino after a meal. (Italians believe that too much milk after a meal is bad for digestion.) If you

can't do without a touch of milk in your espresso, ask for a *caffè macchiato* (literally, "spotted"). For the same with cold milk, ask for a *caffè macchiato freddo.*

The customers at Italian bars will specify the desired temperature (*bollente,* "boiling" or *tiepido,* "lukewarm"), container (*tazza,* "cup," or *al vetro,* "in glass"), and degree of froth (*poca schiuma,* "not much foam") when they order. They also specify volume: *ristretto* is a more concentrated espresso; a *caffè lungo* is made with extra water; a *doppio* is a double espresso. None of these comes anywhere near the large volume or thin consistency of a *caffè americano,* which should be ordered only in large international hotels, if at all.

Espresso spiked with a drop of brandy, grappa, or Sambuca (the Roman anise-flavored liqueur) is called *caffè corretto,* which

In Rome, a frothy *caffelatte* is considered a breakfast drink.

means "corrected." Postprandial coffees are always served after, not with, dessert. A digestif served after (not with) the coffee is called *ammazzacaffè* ("coffee killer").

The word bar in Rome means, first, a coffee bar. But not everyone is addicted to caffeine, or even likes coffee. A *caffè d'orzo* (barley) is a coffeelike brew with the consistency of thin homemade coffee. More often customers will ask for a *decaffeinato* (six syllables) or a Hag (pronounced "ahg"), a popular brand. Bars also serve a range of medicinal-flavored aperitifs and digestifs,

For the complete Roman bar experience, stand at the counter, elbow to elbow with the other patrons. Most bars have two price lists, one for counter service and one for table service. But if you would prefer to sit, don't be put off by the markup for a table. After all, a cup of coffee is a small price to pay when you need a place to rest or meet someone without being hurried away.

Coffee connoisseurs should be sure to visit bars that roast their own beans (look for the word *torrefazione,* which roughly means "roastery"). Unless advertised as 100 percent

If there is one institution that encapsulates the quality of life in Rome, it is the bustling neighborhood coffee bar.

along with the everyday liquors, for which, however, there is less demand. They also offer hot chocolate (mainly a morning drink) and a variety of packaged teas—both caffeinated and decaffeinated.

The secondary business of a bar is to serve assorted other drinks, some alcoholic and some not, and snack foods of vastly varying degrees of interest, from often-limp pastries to the most fascinating arrays of sandwiches and sweets. Occasionally a neighborhood bar will also offer hot food, served cafeteria or even restaurant style. These simple meals can make for a satisfying and inexpensive lunch on the go.

Visitors should make an effort to rise early and have a cappuccino and *cornetto* (the local croissant) with the crowds going to work. Both will taste better and cost much less than a hotel breakfast. But more important, the buzz of activity in the bar hits its peak in the morning, so it's a good idea to stop in early and fuel up, especially if you plan to spend the rest of the day walking around the city and standing in museums and churches, which can be quite exhausting.

arabica, the coffee itself is probably a *miscela* (blend) of arabica and robusta beans, as many people like the kick and extra caffeine of robusta. Popular national coffee brands that appear frequently in Roman bars include Lavazza, from Turin; Kimbo, from Naples; and Illy Caffè, which comes from Trieste.

Every Rome guidebook mentions the tiny, always crowded Caffè Sant'Eustachio, with its extracreamy espresso, and the historic Tazza d'Oro, both near the Pantheon. Caffè Sant'Eustachio is known for serving coffee already sweetened with plenty of sugar. If you prefer no sugar, you have to say so up front. Both bars make outstanding coffee granitas topped with *panna montata* (whipped cream).

Many bars are just as busy, but not quite as famous. Cafffè Camerino (with three f's), on Largo Argentina, is practically an archetype. Loyal clientele from the neighborhood flock there for coffee beans (freshly ground or whole), sweets of all kinds to take home, superb sandwiches, and a profusion of chocolate Easter eggs or whatever is in season. Most important, the *baristi* know how to make an excellent coffee.

Alberto Sordi, playing a would-be American in the film *Un Americano a Roma* (1954), eyes his mother's spaghetti and growls, "Maccherone, m'hai provocato . . . e io me te magno." (Pasta, you've gotten on my nerves . . . and I'm gonna scarf you down.) The hero then abandons himself to pleasure.

PASTA

Alberto Sordi was the quintessential Roman actor, and his great genius was his ability to embody the postwar everyman. In the much-loved scene quoted above, the Romans laugh with him, not at him. Now, as then, pasta is what you eat at mamma's kitchen table and also what you order at a fancy restaurant. It's what makes a meal a meal. All pretense collapses before it.

Countless other foods are at its service. Vegetables—zucchini (courgettes), artichokes, various broccolis—have a double life as pasta sauces when sautéed with garlic and a little chile. The sauce from *coda alla vaccinara* (page 143) may be even more delicious the next day served over *tonnarelli* (fresh square-cut spaghetti). Ricotta and spinach achieve harmony as the stuffing for ravioli. Beans and chickpeas (garbanzo beans) are often mixed

with pasta to make some of Rome's favorite dishes, such as *pasta e ceci* (page 93).

Pasta varies in composition, shape, and manufacture. It can be fresh or dried, made with or without eggs. The dough may be rolled and cut (by hand or machine) or extruded through dies. The flour can be *grano tenero* (soft wheat), *grano duro* or *semola* (hard wheat), or other grains: *grano saraceno* (buckwheat), *farro* (emmer), *riso* (rice), and *mais* (corn). Shapes can be long or short, and different types call for different sauces.

When making fettuccine and other pasta at home, it helps to have a hand-cranked machine that rolls and cuts the dough into neat strips. Some traditional homemade pastas, however, are made by hand. These include odd shapes such as *strozzapreti* (priest stranglers) and *stracci* (rags).

Most Roman neighborhoods have a little shop that sells freshly-made fettuccine, *tonnarelli*, tortellini, ravioli, and—especially on Thursdays—gnocchi. Many of these shops also offer a small selection of packaged dried pastas and sauce ingredients. Some pasta makers draw their customers from all over Rome with their original creations. Grand Gourmet, in the Flaminio quarter north of the center, is known for jumbo *tortelli*, stuffed with, among other things, cheese and pears or *speck* (cured, smoked pork flank) and radicchio. Cellini, in the modern EUR quarter, sells specialties of other regions, such as *vincisgrassi* (a sort of lasagne), typical of the Marche, and *stringozzi* (long thick pasta) from Umbria. Franciosi, in the Appio quarter just outside the walls, is known for gnocchi flavored with *ortiche* (nettles).

For Romans, a meal without pasta is like a day without sunshine.

The world of pasta does not split neatly into industrial and homemade. Many shops selling fresh pasta rely on a method that falls somewhere between the two. Large machines are typically used to mix, extrude, and roll the dough, but it is often shaped and finished by hand.

Choosing Pasta

The starting point for choosing a good dried pasta is the label. The best pasta is made in Italy of only semolina flour and water and has been extruded through *trafile di bronzo* (bronze dies), which gives it a rough surface that helps it absorb the sauce. If dried pasta is bright yellow, it has probably been extruded through plastic or Teflon dies. Many artisanal or small manufacturers, such as Latini and Benedetto Cavalieri, slow dry their pasta at low temperatures, which adds to the quality.

Who Invented Pasta?

Grain was first cultivated some nine thousand years ago. It was only a matter of time before someone thought to grind it into flour, mix it with water, shape it, and dry it.

Al-Idrisi, the Arab court geographer to Roger II of Sicily, reported in 1138 that the residents of Trabia, near Palermo, dried and exported strands of dough they called *itriya,* Arabic for "string." Records from Genoa dated 1244 and from the Anjou court in Naples dated 1295 show similar activity.

By the mid-fourteenth century, the Bolognese tradition of fresh pasta was under way. Then, in the 1830s, the modern age of dried commercial pasta began in Naples, along with the practice of cooking it al dente and serving it with a tomato sauce. Experimentation with shapes began early. Dozens of antique pasta machines, as well as the shapes they made, are on display at the small pasta museum, the Museo Nazionale delle Paste Alimentari, near the Quirinal Palace.

Making Tortelloni

MIXING Equal amounts of soft-wheat and hard-wheat flours, a little salt, and eggs are mixed together by machine and then kneaded for about ten minutes. Water is added—just enough for the dough to form walnut-sized balls.

ROLLING The dough is shifted to a second compartment in the machine, from which it is extruded and spooled onto rollers. Sheets are cut from the spooled dough. They are passed through a second machine for rolling, emerging about three times longer and nearly paper-thin. Pieces

of *speck* (smoke-cured pork) are put through a meat grinder and mixed with mascarpone and Parmigiano-Reggiano cheeses to make the filling.

FILLING AND SHAPING A pasta sheet is trimmed to a neat rectangle, brushed with egg yolk, and scored into squares. A dollop of filling is placed on each square, the squares are cut apart, each square is folded into a triangle, and the edges are pressed to seal. Finally, the two far points of the triangle are brought together, while the third point is curled outward like the peak of a soft cap.

TORTELLONI

BUCATINI

CAPPELLETTI

MALTAGLIATI

TORTELLONI

In Rome, ravioli are usually square and filled with a spinach and ricotta mixture, while *agnolotti,* usually semicircular, are filled with meat. Handmade stuffed pastas in less conventional shapes and extra-large sizes are called *tortelli* or *tortelloni.* A fluffy ricotta filling is perfect with the extra-tender pasta of *tortelloni,* though the form also lends itself to creative fillings, such as pear and cheese or radicchio and *speck.* Like ravioli, *tortelloni* can be served with a simple tomato sauce or with melted butter, sage leaves, and freshly grated Parmigiano-Reggiano.

BUCATINI

Bucatini are thick spaghetti pierced down the middle by a narrow hole. What good is such a small hole? The risk with any thick shape is that the outside could cook to a mush while the inside remains crunchy. The hole allows the water to penetrate to the core so the pasta will cook evenly. In Rome, *bucatini* are almost always served *all'amatriciana* or *alla gricia.* They are difficult to eat with dignity: meant to be twirled like spaghetti, the strands fight back by hurling flecks of tomato sauce at the diner's shirt.

CAPPELLETTI

Christmas isn't Christmas without a full-bodied capon broth and plenty of small, meat-filled *cappelletti.* The name means "little hats," with specific reference to a type of floppy medieval hat. The shape is usually associated with the tortellini of the Emilia-Romagna region, where it originated. Technically the dough for *cappelletti* is a bit more robust and the exact composition of the meat filling varies. *Cappelletti* used to be eaten frequently with rich cream sauces, but today they are usually found only in broth.

MALTAGLIATI

The neat rhomboids into which commercially made *maltagliati* are cut belie their name, which means "badly cut." There are two kinds of *maltagliati,* those cut neatly but on the bias, either manufactured or homemade, and those truer to their name, the scraps of any kind of pasta dough left over after ravioli, fettuccine, and lasagne have been cut into their uniform shapes. Both types can be cooked and sauced as for any short pasta shape, but in Rome they are often mixed with legumes in hearty soups such as *pasta e ceci* (page 93).

ORECCHIETTE

Although this shape, called "little ears," is associated with the south of Italy, it is quite popular in Rome. The dough is made from either all hard-wheat flour, or half hard and half soft wheat, and water. Neither extruded nor rolled and cut, they represent a third technique of pasta making: rolling and poking. Small handfuls are pulled from a ball of dough and rolled into cylinders, which are cut into small pieces. Each piece is poked with a thumb and drawn against the work surface until concave. *Broccoletti* (page 45) are their natural partner.

PENNE

Penna means "quill," and it is easy to see where bias-cut penne get their name. The short pasta can be found both smooth surfaced (*liscie*) and ridged (*rigate*). This versatile shape almost certainly migrated north from Campania, but penne are probably Rome's most popular all-purpose dried short pasta, often tossed with vegetable-based sauces such as *broccolo romanesco* (page 44), asparagus, or artichokes. They are obligatory in the dish *penne all'arrabbiata*, a simple but delicious Roman specialty of tomatoes, garlic, chile, and parsley.

RIGATONI

A major player in the world of short formats, rigatoni are characterized by a large hole, a half inch (12 mm) or more in diameter. Relatively thick and sturdy, they take about twice as long to cook as spaghetti. They get their name from the striations—*riga* means "straight line"—that cover the outer surface. Rigatoni are well suited to sauces that combine solids and liquid. In Rome, the typical condiment is a tomato sauce with *la pagliata*, the intestines of a milk-fed calf. *Mezzemaniche* and *bombolotti* are similar, but shorter, shapes popular in Rome.

SPAGHETTI

When you tie up a package, you use *spago* (twine), and indeed spaghetti are nothing more than strings of hard-wheat flour and water. The king of pasta shapes, spaghetti can range in diameter from 1.7 to 2 milimeters (less than 1/16 inch). Any less and a second diminutive suffix turns it into *spaghettini*. Spaghetti is at its best with oil-based or relatively thin sauces that easily coat the long strands, such as *alle vongole* (with clams) or *pomodoro e basilico* (with tomato and basil).

ORECCHIETTE

PENNE

RIGATONI

SPAGHETTI

Wild borage, deep-green chard, crisp lettuces, pink-tinged spinach, crunchy *puntarelle,* and an abundance of broccolis and chicories—the array of greens (and reds, yellows, and oranges) makes the Roman vegetable markets among the most exciting sights in a city hardly lacking in visual interest.

GREENS

Most Romans like broccoli—and *broccoletti*—and spinach, chard, cauliflower, and Brussels sprouts. It is not a chore to get people to eat their vegetables. Greens just taste better in Rome. They are sweeter—milder and yet more flavorful at the same time. That is true whether the greens are homegrown or brought in from warmer regions, including Sicily, Sardinia, Puglia, and Campania.

Still, produce grown near Rome, which bears the label *romanesco,* is considered the most desirable. Until well into the 1980s, one of the most striking features as you drove out of Rome was the abrupt switch from urban center to rural area. That rapidly shrinking countryside, the immediate outskirts of Rome, especially extending to the southeast into the Alban Hills, is the *campagna romana,* immortalized in generations of Grand Tour paintings

typically populated by peasants in colorful clothes with aprons, brimmed hats, and baskets. Their spiritual, and in some cases actual, descendants—unfortunately fewer and fewer of them—still gather wild chicories, cresses, lettuces, borage, and herbs to sell in town at the large and small municipal markets that serve every neighborhood. Urban sprawl, however, is taking its toll.

Rome's splendid climate, which can hover above freezing for at most a few weeks each winter, but rarely goes below it, produces magnificent leafy greens, both domesticated and wild, all winter. Wild salad greens, sold collectively as *misticanza* or *insalata di campo* (field greens), are hand gathered by sharp-eyed, experienced pickers. While globalization and greenhouses make produce like strawberries and tomatoes available year-round, the

offerings at the city markets punctuate the seasons better than any calendar. When the big, round artichokes from Cerveteri, just north of Rome, ease out the smaller Sardinians in March, it's time to think about making *carciofi alla giudia* (page 52), and then in a few weeks *la vignarola* (page 94), because fava (broad) beans and peas will be coming along. Asparagus are available year-round nowadays, but their peak season is still spring. The beautiful fluted *zucchine romanesche* are in the markets by late winter, but smart shoppers hold off, because when the weather turns torrid, zucchini (courgettes), eggplants (aubergines), and bell peppers (capsicums) become the pillars of the local cuisine. In summer, Rome is filled with tomatoes, which are cooked into sauces or eaten raw in salads.

A wealth of greens and other vegetables nourishes Romans year-round.

**CICORIA
SELVATICA**

MISTICANZA ROMANA

BROCCOLO ROMANESCO

LATTUGA ROMANA

BROCCOLO ROMANESCO

The Roman variety of what in Italian is properly called *cavolo broccolo romanesco* is found principally in the winter. It looks like a chartreuse cauliflower with strange pointed florets, but the taste is nearer broccoli. The florets are delicious simply boiled or steamed and dressed with olive oil and a squeeze of lemon or deep-fried as part of a *fritto misto*. They can also be boiled and sautéed, like *cicoria* and *broccoletti,* or served on pasta. The most emblematic use of *broccolo* in Roman cooking is in *minestra di arzilla con pasta e broccoli*—skate broth with *broccolo* and spaghetti.

CICORIA SELVATICA

Gathered in the countryside in the cooler months, wild chicory grows in exuberant heads with lots of almost-curly, saw-toothed leaves. The flavor ranges from pleasantly bitter to very bitter indeed. The leaves should be rinsed and trimmed like spinach and then dropped into a large pot of boiling salted water and cooked until quite tender. In Rome, those with strong palates will eat boiled chicory cold with olive oil and lemon juice, but most people prefer to sauté the boiled greens with garlic and chile.

MISTICANZA ROMANA

The term *misticanza* is regularly applied to various assortments of greens, from mild combinations that recall Provençal mesclun to banal bags of ready-made salads to robust blends of spiky, hairy wild things that must be boiled to be edible. To connoisseurs, however, *la misticanza romana* is a wild salad of considerable character and exquisite charm. The mix, gathered in the countryside in wintertime, will vary, but may include chicory, salad burnet, wood sorrel, borage, endive, and poppy greens. It is usually dressed with only vinegar and olive oil.

LATTUGA ROMANA

American Caesar salad is creeping onto Italian menus—and no wonder, with such tender and flavorful romaine (cos) lettuce. In Rome, it is called simply *lattuga* (lettuce). In the vernacular of the Roman vegetable market, the generic term for salad greens is *insalata* rather than *lattuga*, which is reserved for romaine only. It is used as any salad green, but unlike other lettuces, it can also be cooked, as an addition to *la vignarola* (page 94), or braised on its own and served as a *contorno*.

BROCCOLETTI

RUGHETTA SELVATICA

SPINACI

PUNTARELLE

BROCCOLETTI

Broccoletti are not exactly the same thing as broccoli rabe, which is *cime di rapa* or *broccoletti di rapa.* But they are so similar that the slight differences don't matter. The plant, available principally in the cooler months, is like broccoli whose leaves have grown and whose florets have shrunk. Greengrocers carefully trim off the tough ends, then peel and split the remaining stems. *Broccoletti* make an excellent addition to pasta, or they can be served as a side dish, boiled and dressed with olive oil and lemon juice.

RUGHETTA SELVATICA

In Italian it is *ruchetta,* in Rome it is *rughetta selvatica.* Although best translated as "wild arugula," a truly analogous plant may not exist outside Italy. Available all year, *rughetta* has a bitter, peppery flavor. Despite the name, most of the *rughetta selvatica* sold is cultivated, but sharp eyes will find it growing even in the city. It's often mixed with cherry tomatoes or with other greens for a salad, but is delicious on its own, too, or combined with sliced green (spring) onions and shaved Parmigiano-Reggiano.

SPINACI

People who think they don't like spinach should not give up until they have tasted it in Italy. Mainly available in winter, it reaches the market young and tender, enticingly pink at the base of the stems, the smallest leaves almost emerald. The whole leaves are usually steamed and then served with butter or with lemon and olive oil. It can also be sautéed with raisins and pine nuts. Spinach is an essential ingredient in classic ravioli when mixed with ricotta. The smallest leaves are often separated out and sold for salads.

PUNTARELLE

The fresh, slightly bitter taste of this *romanissima* salad green is reason enough to visit the Eternal City in winter. With the first warm weather, the stalks of *puntarelle,* a type of Catalonian chicory, grow woody, and won't be seen again until the first chill of autumn. In Rome, *puntarelle* are always served with a dressing made with anchovy and garlic (page 160). Preparation begins with the special cut. The outer leaves and tough bases of the hollow stalks are removed. Each stalk is then carefully peeled and split lengthwise into several steps.

A crisp focaccia with prosciutto, a six-foot-long (2 meter) flat bread, a rectangle of dough strewn with sliced potatoes, a canapé, a cherry pie, and a round crust with tomatoes and mozzarella: in Rome, they all come under the term *pizza*.

PIZZA

In the relatively rigid program that represents the Italian gastronomic day or week, pizza is usually the main item in a light sit-down meal served in a dedicated pizzeria. It is usually washed down with beer, soda, or a light white wine and may be preceded by bruschetta (page 69), *suppli* (page 73), deep-fried salt-cod fillets, or other snacks, usually fried. When the pizzeria also serves other dishes, the pizza may be treated as a *primo piatto,* that is, a substitute for pasta or soup.

On Sunday evenings, Rome's pizzerias are filled with families. The rest of the week, the customers tend to be young people who want to *stare insieme* (pass the time together), or groups of adults who want an evening out that is not *impegnativo* (a big commitment).

The best pizzas come from wood-burning ovens, which are rarely fired up before dark in Rome's warm climate, making it easier to find a pizza for dinner than for lunch. The Roman crust is thin and fairly crisp, though tender enough to be eaten—as is proper—with knife and fork. The border is narrow and low. As with pasta, the crust should not be viewed as merely a vehicle for the topping. A naked pizza—the Roman focaccia—drizzled with olive oil and perhaps adorned with some diced tomatoes or a slice or two of prosciutto, is proof of that.

The yeasty Neapolitan crust, with its wide, high border, has been making inroads in Rome, but this is probably the only identifiably external influence. Pizza toppings include old classics, new classics, and idiosyncrasies of individual pizzerias. Pies topped with *mozzarella di bufala* and Pachino tomatoes (prized cherry tomatoes from southeastern Sicily), *fiori di zucca* (zucchini/courgette flowers), or *rughetta* (arugula/rocket) have joined *pizza alla napoletana* (anchovies, tomatoes, and mozzarella), *pizza ai funghi* (fresh mushrooms, tomatoes, and mozzarella), and *pizza Margherita* (tomatoes, mozzarella, and sometimes basil) as near-universal menu items.

One of the best places in Rome to find thin-crust pizza is Da Baffetto, near Piazza Navona. At Pizzeria Ivo in Trastevere, pizzas come in two sizes (large and larger), and a trattoria menu is also available. Both Da Baffetto and Ivo have plenty of atmosphere, but for the quintessential Roman pizzeria experience—lots of bustle, no-frills decor, outdoor seating in summer, and a great thin crust—you can't beat Ai Marmi, also in Trastevere, known popularly as "*l'obitorio*" (the morgue) because of its marble tables.

Naples invented it, but Rome has perfected thin-crust pizza.

High on the list of things that make Romans proud is *pizza bianca*—literally, "white pizza"—the sublime flat bread that is white and soft inside and golden brown and crisp on top. When the pizza is filled with ripe figs and prosciutto, a local favorite, it is called *pizza e fichi*, a term that has come to mean "as good as it gets" in local parlance.

Popular Fillings

Pizza bianca is often eaten plain, preferably just out of the oven, but almost every snack bar in town offers it split horizontally and filled as a sandwich. Most Romans like it stuffed with ripe fresh figs and prosciutto. But the fig season is short. *Mortadella* or prosciutto and fresh mozzarella is a classic, while *bresaola* and *rughetta* (arugula/rocket), with or without shaved Parmigiano-Reggiano, is decidedly modern. Tuna and marinated artichoke hearts is another time-tested combination.

Where to Find Pizza Bianca

Just about every *panificio* (bakery) in town bakes *pizza bianca* and every corner store sells it and will fill it with something easy. Shops that serve *pizza al taglio* (by the slice) often also sell *pizza bianca* filled with sautéed greens or other ingredients. Two good ones to try are Pizzeria Leonina, on the street of the same name near Via Cavour, and Pizzeria Florida, on Largo Argentina. But true aficionados go to the shops that specialize in p*izza bianca* cut and filled to order.

At Frontoni, on Viale Trastevere, no one will bat an eyelash at unusual requests. *Puntarelle* paired with salami? Eggplant (aubergine) and smoked mozzarella? No problem. Roscioli, on Via dei Chiavari, fills its superb pizza with simpler fare, such as *bresaola*. Finally, the famed Antico Forno in Piazza Campo de' Fiori opened a separate shop to sell its ready-stuffed gourmet *pizza bianca* with fillings such as zucchini (courgette) flowers and mozzarella.

Making Pizza Bianca

MIXING For each batch of *pizza bianca,* flour, water, salt, and cake yeast are put into a giant mixer, which first combines the ingredients and then kneads them to yield a smooth, elastic dough. The dough is left to rise for up to 6 hours.

SHAPING AND KNEADING The risen dough is cut into portions each weighing about 4 pounds (2 kg). Each piece is shaped by hand into a 24-inch (60-cm) loaf, sprinkled with flour, and left to rest for about 15 minutes. The loaves are then kneaded and stretched. After the dough is worked

for about 5 minutes, it emerges as a slim shape approximately 6 feet (2 m) long. The pizza's characteristic dimpled surface is made by the baker's fingertips, which work over the surface as if they were playing a piano.

BAKING The pizzas are brushed with olive oil and transferred on a long, narrow *pala* (peel) to the oven, where they bake at 500°F (260°C) for 10 minutes until crisp and golden. They are then slipped onto a shelf and left to cool.

Artichokes plunged into hot oil, zucchini (courgette) flowers filled with mozzarella, deep-fried salt-cod fillets, and ricotta desserts are all associated with the traditional table of Rome's Jewish community. Today, these dishes are almost inseparable from the popular cooking of the city.

CUCINA EBRAICA

A Jewish community has existed in Rome since at least the second century BC. The population numbered perhaps forty thousand at the height of the Roman Empire. Many Jews were brought to Rome as slaves captured in wars in Judaea in the first century AD. They lived in various parts of the city, especially in Trastevere. In the thirteenth century, the city's Jews were segregated in a few blocks opposite the Tiber Island. Then, in 1555, a papal edict forced them to live within a ghetto with gates kept locked at night. It also mandated the closure of all but one synagogue, curtailed their civil rights, and severely limited their means of making a living. The gates remained until 1848.

La cucina ebraica, or "Jewish cooking," in the Roman context refers to the recipes developed by the small group of city dwellers who lived in this tiny, densely populated neighborhood. Within the limits of their dietary laws and their poverty (shared with much of Rome), Jewish cooks are generally credited with having invented the city's *cucina povera* (peasant cooking). Deep-frying, still today the downfall of many Romans, gave flavor to ingredients that the wealthy spurned, like zucchini (courgette) flowers. Traditional recipes now seldom found outside the home include *indivia rehaminà* (chicory/curly endive soup), *scaloppine con la lattuga* (veal with romaine/cos lettuce), and stuffed turkey neck. Other dishes, such as red mullet with raisins and pine nuts, considered a delicacy, and fresh anchovies baked with chicory, do sometimes appear on restaurant menus.

Today, the Jewish quarter—it is still there, and is very desirable real estate—is home to a concentration of food shops and restaurants, though not all of them are kosher or even Jewish. Gentile Rome goes to the Ghetto, too, for outstanding kosher *pizza al taglio* (by the slice) and *panini* at Zi' Fenizia and for superb *torta di ricotta* (page 170) and *tozzetti* (page 173) at the Forno del Ghetto, the tiny bakery on Via del Portico d'Ottavia.

The most popular dishes from the *cucina ebraica* today are the *fritti:* deep-fried artichokes, zucchini flowers, salt-cod fillets, and bites of mozzarella and vegetables. In the quarter, elegant Piperno and venerable Da Giggetto, located right next to the ancient ruins of the Portico d'Ottavia, both serve excellent Jewish-Roman cuisine. Across the Tiber, in Trastevere, Ristorante Paris (a surname, not an allusion to France) produces an irresistible Jewish-style *fritto misto.*

The tiny Forno del Ghetto is famous for its cinnamon *tozzetti*.

Perhaps the most famous dish of the Roman Jewish repertory is *carciofo alla giudia,* a deep-fried artichoke that is pressed flat until it resembles a flower dipped in bronze. The petals are crisp, which makes the tender heart almost a surprise. There's no batter or flour. The magic is in the expert preparation of the artichoke so that every bit is edible.

Artichoke Varieties

Carciofo alla giudia achieves its greatest glory in late winter and early spring with the arrival of the Romanesco artichoke, a globe variety harvested around Rome. It is even better if it's also a *cimarolo,* from the *cima* (top) of the plant's main stem. *Cimaroli* are larger than the artichokes from the side branches, and the top is slightly flattened. During most of winter, Rome's markets offer delicious, albeit smaller, specimens from warmer regions.

Fritti

Rome has a mass addiction to deep-frying. Morsels of food, some in *pastella* (batter), some in bread crumbs, and some thrown naked into the hot oil, are served in various combinations at every level of the restaurant hierarchy. Bars, *rosticcerie, friggitorie* (fry shops), and pizzerias serve *supplì* (page 73), and *arancini* (rice balls). A typical *fritti* lineup will feature, in addition to artichokes, batter-dipped zucchini (courgette) flowers filled with mozzarella and anchovies, nutmeg-scented potato croquettes, and crisp zucchini spears. It is usually a good idea to skip the fried snacks at neighborhood pizzerias and order them instead at gourmet shops or fine restaurants. The *supplì* offered at the cafeteria-style Volpetti Più, in Testaccio, are excellent, as are the *fritti* at Checco er Carettiere, in Trastevere. But good *fritti* are not confined to fancy establishments: the best *baccalà* (salt cod) fillets are at Filettaro Santa Barbara, which serves almost nothing else.

Making Carciofi alla Giudia

TRIMMING One of the most enviable skills of the Roman cook or greengrocer is the ability to trim a raw artichoke into a neat ball atop a smooth stem, all edible. The outer leaves are pulled off, and the stem is peeled. The artichoke is then rolled against a blade to remove the tips of the outer layer. Finally, the center leaves and choke are dug out, and the artichokes are placed in water.

FRYING The damp artichokes are tossed vigorously with salt and pepper and dropped into a deep pot of hot (330°–350°F/170°–180°C) olive oil for about 20 minutes, then drained head down. Just before serving, the fried artichokes are dropped into fresh hot oil for a brief second fry.

PRESSING After the second fry, each artichoke is pressed gently, head down, between perforated metal disks to drain off the last drops of oil. This gives the artichoke its characteristic flowerlike shape. From there, it goes directly to the plate, alone or as part of a *fritto misto*.

Gone are the days when the local carafe wine curled your hair and most bottles either had a screw cap or came from Tuscany. It is getting easier and easier to find good wine in Rome. Today, chic wine shops and wine bars with encyclopedic lists have largely replaced neighborhood barrel-and-carafe hangouts.

WINE

The wines produced in Lazio, the region around Rome, are 80 percent white, and almost all of the whites contain the native Trebbiano and Malvasia grapes. Led by Frascati, the most famous local appellation, Lazio's white wines have always been known for being low cost and easy to drink. Until the 1990s, they were rarely noted for their quality, but thanks to the efforts of a few dedicated producers, local whites are now poured in some of Rome's finest restaurants. Reds from the region, relying largely on either Sangiovese or international grape varieties, have also won greater recognition in recent years.

In Rome, it is popular for new, hip wine establishments to go by the English term *wine bar,* rather than the traditional *fiaschetteria, bottiglieria,* or *osteria.* In the past, Italian towns boasted neighborhood places where

patrons came to drink wine and socialize. The wine was drawn by spigot from barrels into glass carafes, and the available food was often just enough to keep the drinker upright—say, a hard-boiled egg. These places have evolved into elite operations serving interesting wines from every region in Italy, and even abroad, plus light meals and snacks.

Two excellent wine bars that led the way are Cavour 313, on Via Cavour near the Roman Forum, and Cul de Sac, in Piazza Pasquino, near Piazza Navona. The 'Gusto complex, in Piazza Augusto Imperatore, combines a pizzeria, cookware shop, and restaurant with a state-of-the-art wine bar. The first of the modern wine bars, Trimani, on Via Cernaia, near Termini station, is an adjunct to the adjacent wine shop of the same name. Anacleto Bleve's new wine bar, Casa

Bleve, near Piazza Navona, started almost by accident when he began serving a casual lunch at his older shop, located in the Ghetto.

There are three official quality designations for Italian wine. *Denominazione d'origine controllata* (DOC), is the basic designation, corresponding to the *appellation contrôlée* in France. It guarantees that the wine was both produced within a designated area and in keeping with specific criteria of composition and production. *Denominazione d'origine controllata e Garantita* (DOCG) is similar, with stricter controls. In the past, producers who found the DOC designation too restrictive had to label their bottles *vino da tavola* (table wine). Since 1992, *indicazione geografica tipica* (IGT) has provided a category for diverse blends and techniques tied to a specific area, but with less rigid specifications.

Both the red and white wines of Lazio have finally come into their own.

FRASCATI

MARINO DOC

EST! EST!! EST!!!
DI MONTEFIASCONE

CERVETERI

FRASCATI

Until the 1990s, straw-colored Frascati DOC, a blend of native Malvasia and Trebbiano grapes, was considered an inexpensive, drinkable wine. Its fame depended on its sheer quantitative dominance of the region's production and on the beauty of the hill towns of the Castelli Romani, southeast of Rome, where the vineyards flourish. Many of its producers still go for quantity—now aided by modern techniques that make a drier, more uniform wine—but the single-vineyard Frascatis of some estates, such as Castel de Paolis and Villa Simone, are lovely—both floral and fruity.

MARINO DOC

Another DOC zone in the Castelli Romani, the Marino area produces wines that are similar in composition to adjacent Frascati. The zone is dominated by two names. One is the large, and largely mass-market, Gotta d'Oro. The other is the family business that put the Castelli on the modern enological map, Colle Picchioni, founded in the 1970s by Paola Di Mauro. She and her son Armando still run the business. Bright gold Colle Picchioni Selezione Oro, a blend of Malvasia del Lazio, Trebbiano Giallo, Sémillon, and small amounts of other grapes, has notes of acacia flowers and apples.

EST! EST!! EST!!! DI MONTEFIASCONE

This DOC white from the province of Viterbo is made of Trebbiano, Malvasia, and Rossetto grapes. It is best known for its funny name, born of legend: in 1100, a German bishop traveling to Rome sent his servant ahead to find inns with wine fit to drink. He was to write "est" (Latin for "it is") on the door of acceptable inns. At Montefiascone, the servant found the wine to be so good that he wrote his recommendation in triplicate. Falesco's single-vineyard Poggio dei Gelsi, along with a few others, has brought dignity back to the denomination.

CERVETERI

Cerveteri is the name of a charming town north of Rome, near the Tyrrhenian Sea. It is a DOC zone and, perhaps most famously, an archaeological area containing historically important and beautiful Etruscan cemeteries. Wines have been produced in the area for hundreds of years, and the Etruscan method of training vines to trees, called *vite maritata,* is still found in parts of central Italy. The DOC designation covers both white and red, but the white (made from 50 percent Trebbiano grapes, 35 percent Malvasia, and smaller amounts of other varieties) is prevalent.

GRECHETTO

The Grechetto grape, one of central Italy's oldest varieties, is usually associated with Umbria but grows well in northeastern Lazio. The award-winning Latour a Civitella, produced by Sergio Mottura and classified as Grechetto di Civitella d'Agliano IGT, is made entirely from Grechetto grapes grown near the town of Civitella d'Agliano, almost in Umbria. The bright gold wine is fermented in wood casks in ancient grottoes of volcanic tufa before spending ten more months in oak. More often Grechetto is mixed with Trebbiano, Verdello, and Malvasia, other native whites.

ROSSO LAZIO

The designation Rosso Lazio IGT is used for some of the region's finest and most innovative wines. The Di Mauro family's Vigna del Vassallo, a velvety Merlot blend, has earned "Three Glasses" (the maximum) in the prestigious *Gambero Rosso* classification. Other respected Lazio IGTs include Castel de Paolis's I Quattro Mori, made of Shiraz, Merlot, Cabernet Sauvignon, and Petit Verdot; and Casale del Giglio's Mater Matuta, mostly Shiraz with 15 percent Petit Verdot. Falesco's Montiano is all Merlot, a favorite component of new Lazio reds.

CESANESE

Many of Lazio's best reds are made from French grape varieties, and others rely primarily on the native Montepulciano or Sangiovese. The local Cesanese grape, however, is used for dry and sweet wines in three DOC zones in the region's southernmost province, Frosinone. The wines, Piglio, Affile, and Olevano Romano, are a lovely ruby red when young. New uses are being found for this ancient grape. Concento IGT, a full-bodied Cesanese-Syrah blend made by L'Olivella, combines the more familiar taste of Syrah with an exotic hint of spiciness.

ALEATICO DI GRADOLI

Frascati and a few other local wines come in semisweet (*abboccato* or *amabile*) versions, but the region's only true dessert wine is the sweet, red Aleatico di Gradoli, from a small DOC zone in the province of Viterbo around the town of Gradoli. Made entirely from the black Aleatico grape, it is often likened to port in its *liquoroso* (fortified) version, accomplished through partially drying the grapes. Its destiny is to be served with hazelnut (filbert) *tozzetti* (page 173), much as Vin Santo is paired with *cantucci* in Tuscany.

If you kept a close eye on a Roman's eating habits, from the first *cornetto* in the morning to the last *cioccolatino* in the evening, you might come away with a new understanding of the words "Mediterranean diet." Every religious holiday and season—indeed, nearly every hour of the day—has its own special *dolce*.

DOLCI

The *pasticceria* (pastry shop) may well be the most important retail establishment in Rome. It is practically the only place where you can buy a last-minute gift on Christmas morning or a gigantic chocolate egg on Easter. The word *dolce*, literally "sweet," covers both the dessert course of the meal and the item itself. The diminutive suffix is attached *(dolcetto)* when a sweet is small or when you are trying to pretend it isn't so sinful. The categories of Roman sweets range from the practically nutritious (biscotti made with milk, suitable for children's breakfasts) to the wicked by any standard, such as *maritozzi*, buns cut in half and filled with whipped cream.

Ever since the earliest history of Rome, when patrician couples shared a spelt cake at their wedding, sweets have been closely associated with religious occasions, and until the eighteenth century, they had to be ordered from convents or made at home. A list of typical Roman confections reads like a liturgical calendar: *colomba* (dove-shaped cake) for Easter, *frappe* (strips of fried dough) for carnival, *maritozzi quaresimali* (raisin buns) for Lent, *pangiallo* (fruitcake) for Christmas, *fave dolci* (almond cookies) for All Souls' Day, and *bignè di San Giuseppe* (cream puffs) for Saint Joseph's Day on March 19, Italy's Father's Day.

Most neighborhoods have a serviceable *pasticceria,* often connected with a bar. In the center of Rome, the elegant *gelateria* Giolitti boasts a big pastry counter of cream puffs and other delicacies. Longer on charm than on polish, the venerable Valzani, in Trastevere, makes more traditional sweets, like *pangiallo* and the spicier *pampepato*, dense cakes bursting with dried fruit and nuts; chewy *mostaccioli;* and *torrone* (nougat) encrusted with pine nuts. I Dolci di Checco er Carettiere, a spiffy new adjunct to an old restaurant near Ponte Sisto, also in Trastevere, makes everything from *cornetti* to éclairs and is also a fashionable place for coffee and snacks, despite its small size. Ciampini, in Piazza San Lorenzo in Lucina, in the heart of the Piazza di Spagna shopping district, provides tables indoors and out for patrons to indulge a sweet tooth, perhaps on miniature cones of gelato.

Every day is February 14 at the colorful and charming Moriondo e Gariglio, between Piazza Collegio Romano and the Pantheon, best known of a growing number of chocolate shops in Rome. (Summertime visitors should know, however, that many chocolate shops close completely for the season.)

Roman sweets vary from crunchy biscotti to fruit-filled tarts.

In the past, when families went on outings to the Castelli Romani, the hill towns southeast of Rome, they would bring their lunch from home. Once in the Castelli, however, they would purchase bread and the various dry *dolci* that went well with a glass of the local sweet wine. The favorites among these sweets were the anise-flavored rings called *ciambelline*.

Ciambelline and Holidays

Ciambelline and the larger *ciambelle* have long figured in a handful of Catholic feast days. On the Feast of the Circumcision, January 1, the Carmelite nuns of Velletri traditionally sent the town magistrate a basket of *ciambelle*. To honor Saint Blaise, patron of wool combers, *ciambelline* are still baked in every town in the province of Rome for his feast day, February 3. French-born Saint Roch is often depicted receiving his only food—a *ciambella*—from a dog.

Ancient Roman Sweets

Ring-shaped sweets have been around at least since the Roman Empire. A recipe for a protodoughnut in Apicius's *De re coquinaria*, the only surviving cookbook of the time, calls for moistening soft bread crumbs with milk, forming the mixture into rings, frying them in oil, and then drizzling with honey.

Cane sugar was imported from Egypt but was far too costly for making sweets. Honey, from local bees or imported from the mountains of Greece, was the ancients' favorite sweetener.

A cooked-down grape must, called *defrutum*, was a popular, and cheaper, alternative.

Flaky pastry and fresh cheese were often combined, a partnership reminiscent of today's honey-drenched Greek and Near Eastern pastries. Largely alien to our modern palates, however, is the ancient custom of combining black pepper with sweet foods, such as fried dates rolled in pepper, and *tyropatina,* a rich custard made of milk, eggs, and honey and a dusting of pepper.

Making Ciambelline al Vino

BEATING THE DOUGH Sugar, olive oil, margarine or other fat, and red wine (though white wine is also an option) are *montati* (beaten) by machine to the consistency of whipped cream. Yeast and cake (soft-wheat) flour are added, and the dough is mixed and then kneaded for about 20 minutes.

ROLLING Knobs of dough are quickly rolled back and forth against the work surface into ropes about 8 inches (20 cm) long and ⅔ inch (1.5 cm) in diameter. Any excess dough is pinched off and returned to the mass of unformed dough. In a single, quick movement, the ends of each rope are gently joined (but not pressed), to form a ring.

DIPPING The resulting ring, about 3½ inches (9 cm) in diameter, is dipped on one side in granulated sugar and set, sugared side up, on a paper-lined baking sheet.

BAKING The *ciambelline* are baked at 425°F (220°C) for 15 to 20 minutes until golden. They are then removed from the oven and left to cool.

CASTAGNACCIO

CORNETTO

CANNOLI

MOSTACCIOLI

CIAMBELLINE AL VINO

CANNOLI

These Sicilian sweets par excellence have been enthusiastically adopted by Romans. They are made from wafers rolled to form large tubes (which *cannoli* roughly means), fried, and then filled with lightly sweetened ricotta. The wafer, called *scorza,* or "rind," contains cocoa and Marsala wine in addition to butter, eggs, and flour. The filling is almost pure ricotta with bits of candied squash *(zuccata),* chocolate, and sometimes pistachios (a product of Sicily). *Mignon,* or "bite-size," cannoli are favorite items in the assortments (usually boxed up to go) that Romans love so much.

CASTAGNACCIO

Castagna (chestnut) flour, sugar, olive oil, raisins, pine nuts, and rosemary go into this dense, flat cake, which resembles a pizza and is more of a snack than a dessert. Children used to buy *castagnaccio* from street vendors. Today, many *pizza al taglio* shops sell it by the slice, although it is also easy to make at home. It is popular in northern Lazio, Umbria, and Tuscany, an important zone for chestnut growing. The sweet is usually prepared in fall and winter, when the nuts are harvested and milled, but it can be made any time of year if the flour has been properly stored to avoid rancidity.

CORNETTO

Cappuccino and *cornetto* are the ritual way to start the Roman day, preferably in a busy bar. In the 1960s, Italian film director Nanni Loy raised the combination to the pantheon of iconic meals on the Italian version of the television show *Candid Camera,* when he dunked his *cornetto* in the cappuccino of strangers to film their astonishment. The shape of the Roman *cornetto* (*corno* means "horn") resembles a croissant, but is usually smaller. It can be filled with jam (usually apricot). A savory version often comes filled with prosciutto.

MOSTACCIOLI

These chewy, diamond-shaped cookies are now found in different versions throughout Italy, but they originated in Lazio. The name is believed to derive from the Latin *mustaceus,* a flat cake consumed at weddings in ancient Rome. *Mustum,* Latin for "grape must" (referring to the juice released before and during fermentation), provided sweetening as well as the name. The ingredients are flour, egg whites, honey, nuts, citrus rind, and candied and dried fruits. Some contemporary versions might include cocoa or chocolate.

CROSTATA DI FRUTTA

PANGIALLO

SFOGLIATELLE

CROSTATA DI FRUTTA

DIAVOLETTI AL PEPERONCINO

CIAMBELLINE AL VINO

Almost anything round can be called a *ciambella,* from a doughnut to a life preserver, so the name tells us that these classic biscotti are going to be small and ring shaped. They are perfect at the end of a meal.

SFOGLIATELLE

Like Marilyn Monroe delighted to find new places to put diamonds, Romans just love new places to put ricotta. These delicacies, which are usually associated with Campania, are made by cutting and layering thin sheets of pastry, which are filled with a creamy combination of ricotta and semolina.

CROSTATA DI FRUTTA

A thick crust of short pastry and a layer of preserved or fresh fruit are all it takes to assemble one of the most popular, and most flexible, of all Roman *dolci.* Sometimes the fruit tart is a quick solution for what to bring to a party; other times it is a showcase for homemade jams cooked from fruits harvested from the bounteous trees of a country house. Bars and pastry shops also offer individual tarts to have with tea, coffee, or perhaps a liqueur. Not traditionally a dessert, the *crostata* is properly eaten as a between-meal snack, often in the late afternoon.

PANGIALLO

The name *pangiallo,* literally "yellow bread," does not do justice to this delicious nut-and-fruit cake, traditionally baked in Lazio and Umbria at Christmastime. It is commonly made with a rich combination of hazelnuts (filberts), walnuts, almonds, pine nuts, raisins, dried figs, candied citron, orange rind, and spices. Like most sweets that can be picked up with the fingers, *pangiallo* is not so much a dessert as something to be enjoyed with coffee or sweet wine. Richer versions used to contain saffron-tinged almond paste, hence the name.

DIAVOLETTI AL PEPERONCINO

Not all Roman sweets have their origin in the mists of time. When the film *Chocolat* suggested the possibilities of chocolate confections flavored with chile, clients of ultra-traditional Valzani in Trastevere began asking for them. Happy to oblige, the *pasticceria* developed a recipe, now patented and secret, for a cocoa-covered tablet that tastes like a chocolate truffle—with a kick that arrives several seconds after the voluptuous filling starts to melt in the mouth. The name, "little devils," refers to the piquancy of the pepper.

ANTIPASTI

Fried zucchini flowers, vinegar-spiked vegetables, or sliced cured

meats—the antipasto is probably the most variable course of the meal.

Nothing seems more typical of the Italian trattoria than a colorful antipasto buffet of marinated fish, grilled vegetables, slices of frittata, and various other savory tidbits. Yet the antipasto course (the word means "before the meal") is not traditional in Rome, which is why rudimentary trattorias often offer nothing more than a plate of prosciutto, perhaps with melon or figs in summer. When paired with rustic Roman bread, most antipasti do double duty as snacks or lunch. Wherever you put them in the meal, a deep-fried *fiore di zucca* or a wedge of frittata spells Rome.

BRUSCHETTA AL POMODORO

Garlic-Rubbed Toast with Fresh Tomatoes and Basil

It seems, and is, so simple—garlic-rubbed toast with raw tomato on top—but like many of the capital city's favorite foods, bruschetta al pomodoro *brings you face to face with the brilliance of basic Roman ingredients. The classic bread for bruschetta is* pane casereccio, *the ordinary Roman loaf, though good hand-sliced sourdough or country bread would be a fine substitute. If you can't find flavorful ripe tomatoes and fresh basil, use none at all, and make the bruschetta with just garlic, salt, and olive oil.*

1 The bread can be toasted on a grill or in a toaster. If using a grill, prepare a charcoal or gas grill for direct grilling over medium-high heat.

2 If using firm salad tomatoes, core them and then slice about ¼ inch (6 mm) thick. If using red, ripe salad tomatoes, core and peel them and then cut into ½-inch (12-mm) dice. If using cherry tomatoes, cut them in half. Tear the larger basil leaves into a few pieces, and leave the smaller leaves whole.

3 If using a grill, lay the bread on the rack about 8 inches (20 cm) above the fire and toast, turning once, until crisp and golden, about 4 minutes total. Alternatively, toast the bread in a toaster. As soon as the bread is ready, rub a whole garlic clove vigorously over one side of it. The rough surface of the bread will shred the garlic like a grater, leaving very little in your hand after 2 slices are rubbed with 1 of the cloves.

4 Divide the bread slices, garlic side up, between 2 plates. Arrange the tomatoes in a single layer on the bread, dividing evenly. If you are using cherry tomatoes, squash the halves, cut side down, into the bread (be careful of squirts). Sprinkle with salt and drizzle generously with the olive oil. Distribute the basil evenly on top. Serve immediately.

Serve with a fruity white wine such as Orvieto Classico.

1 large or 2 medium salad tomatoes or about 16 cherry tomatoes

About 16 fresh basil leaves

4 slices coarse country bread, about ½ inch (12 mm) thick

2 cloves garlic, peeled and left whole

Salt

2–4 tablespoons (1–2 fl oz/ 30–60 ml) extra-virgin olive oil

Makes 2 servings

Breads of Rome

Most Romans will not pick up a fork without a full bread basket on the table. Nor can they finish the meal without bread, since mopping up the last bit of sauce, called *fare la scarpetta,* is standard practice in all but the most formal settings. Even the language divides foods into *pane,* "bread," and everything else, *companatico,* literally "what you put with bread."

Despite the arrival of designer bakeries that feature walnut- and olive-studded loaves, most Romans prefer the old-fashioned chewy *pagnotta,* a round loaf of *pane casereccio* (home-style bread) that can be white or brown and is the traditional choice for bruschetta. Bread baked in wood-fired ovens in the nearby towns of Genzano and Lariano is considered to be among the best in Italy.

Other common loaves are the saltless *tipo Terni,* the airy *napoletano,* and the soft, dense *pane di grano duro.* The basic roll is the hollow, domed *rosetta,* split for a *panino,* but the football-shaped *ciriola,* named for an eel that once swam in the Tiber, and the flat *ciabatta,* or "slipper" loaf, are always available.

ANTIPASTO BIS DI PEPERONI E MELANZANE

Grilled Eggplant and Sweet Peppers

All summer, Roman markets are filled with beautiful eggplants and peppers, trucked in from nearby farms. The eggplants can be chubby and pale violet to white or sleek and near black. The sweet bell peppers are green, yellow, or red and big, often weighing 1 lb (500 g) or more each. This recipe pairs the two vegetables because they both do well on the grill and are happy partners—passed with good bread and perhaps slices of mozzarella di bufala—*at terrazzo parties, but don't hesitate to prepare them separately. Both vegetables also make an excellent side dish.*

FOR THE EGGPLANT

2 cloves garlic

About ½ cup (½ oz/15 g) fresh flat-leaf (Italian) parsley leaves

½ cup (4 fl oz/125 ml) extra-virgin olive oil, or more as needed

1 medium-large eggplant (aubergine), preferably light skinned and round (see note), unpeeled, cut crosswise into slices ⅜ inch (1 cm) thick

2 teaspoons red wine vinegar

Salt, preferably freshly ground

½ teaspoon red pepper flakes (optional)

FOR THE PEPPERS

3 red or yellow bell peppers (capsicums)

2 tablespoons extra-virgin olive oil

1 teaspoon chopped fresh herb such as oregano, Italian (flat-leaf) parsley, or basil (optional)

Salt

Makes 6 servings

1 Prepare a charcoal or gas grill for direct grilling over medium-high heat, or preheat the broiler (grill).

2 Halve the garlic cloves lengthwise and cut away any green shoots. On a cutting board, using a *mezzaluna* (two-handled curved chopping knife), finely chop together the garlic and parsley. (Alternatively, use a chef's knife or a small food processor.) Transfer to a bowl (or work directly in the processor bowl), add the ½ cup olive oil and the vinegar and mix well. Set aside.

3 If grilling, when the coals are ready, lay the peppers and the eggplant slices on the rack about 8 inches (20 cm) above the fire. Grill the peppers, turning as needed, until the skin is evenly blistered on all sides and the flesh is soft but not burned, about 10 minutes total. Cook the eggplant slices, a few at a time if necessary, turning until both sides are marked with brown stripes and are tender, about 6 minutes total. In both cases, the timing will depend on the intensity of the heat.

4 If using the broiler, arrange the eggplant slices on a broiler pan and slip under the broiler about 6 inches (15 cm) from the heat source. Broil (grill), turning once, until lightly browned on both sides and tender, about 4 minutes total, paying closer attention to the color than the clock. Transfer the slices to a flat plate. Place the peppers on the broiler pan and broil, turning as needed, until the skin is evenly blistered and charred, about 10 minutes total; watch carefully to avoid burning their flesh.

5 At this point, the destiny of each vegetable diverges. Put the peppers into a paper bag, close the top, and set aside until cool enough to handle. Then remove them from the bag, cut off the stem end and a thin slice from the base of each pepper, and pull off all the skin that comes away easily. Slit each pepper open lengthwise and remove and discard the seeds. Using a small, sharp knife, peel away any remaining skin. Don't worry if some small patches won't come off. Cut lengthwise into strips about ⅜ inch (1 cm) wide. As you work, cut away the ribs and flick away any tenacious seeds. Put the pepper strips in a small serving bowl, dress with the olive oil, and sprinkle with the herb, if using, before serving.

6 Let the eggplant slices cool slightly. Select a straight-sided glass or ceramic serving dish just large enough to hold the slices tightly packed. Layer the slices with the olive oil–parsley mixture, and top each layer with a little salt and with a few red pepper flakes, if using. If the eggplant seems dry, add more oil.

7 The peppers and eggplant can be covered and left at room temperature for up to 1 hour or kept in the refrigerator for up to 3 days. Bring the vegetables to room temperature before serving.

Serve with an aromatic white wine such as a Mueller-Thurgau from Alto Adige or a local Frascati Superiore.

SUPPLÌ AL TELEFONO

Rice Croquettes

The word supplì *supposedly derives from the French* surprise, *and refers to the core of molten mozzarella at the heart of this popular egg-shaped croquette, a ubiquitous appetizer in Roman pizzerias. Why* telefono? *When the* supplì *is bitten into and one half is pulled away from the other, the cheese forms a long string, which suggests, after a fashion, the cord linking the receiver and the base of a telephone. Despite the allusion, most Romans resist the temptation to make smart remarks about the city's sometimes "surprising" phone service or the arrival of cordless technology.*

1 To make the tomato mixture, in a small bowl, combine the mushrooms with warm water to cover and let stand for 15 minutes to rehydrate. Drain, squeeze out the excess liquid, and chop finely. In a frying pan over medium heat, warm the olive oil. Add the beef, onion, and mushrooms and sauté until the meat is no longer red, about 10 minutes. Add the tomato purée and ½ teaspoon salt, bring to a boil, reduce the heat to medium-low, and simmer, uncovered, until the sauce has reduced by about one-third, about 20 minutes. Remove from the heat and set aside to cool.

2 To make the rice, bring a large saucepan three-fourths full of water to a rapid boil over high heat. Add 1 tablespoon salt and the rice and cook, stirring occasionally with a wooden spoon, until the rice has softened but is still al dente, 10–12 minutes. Drain the rice and spread it out on a large platter or roasting pan to cool slightly. Add the eggs, butter, cheese, a pinch of salt, and the tomato mixture. Using your hands, mix to combine. Let cool to room temperature.

3 To form the croquettes, whisk the egg in a small, shallow bowl until blended. Pour the bread crumbs into a second shallow bowl. Using a soupspoon, scoop up some rice and form into a ball the size and shape of an egg. Using an index finger, make an indentation in the side of the ball, insert a piece of the mozzarella deep into the center, and close the rice around it. Roll the ball in the beaten egg to coat evenly, and then roll in the bread crumbs, again coating evenly. Place the ball on a large, flat plate or tray. Repeat with the remaining rice and cheese, evenly coating each ball. When all the balls are formed, cover the plate and refrigerate the balls for at least 1 hour or for up to overnight before cooking.

4 Preheat the oven to 150°F (65°C) and put an ovenproof platter in it. To cook the croquettes, pour olive oil to a depth of at least 2 inches (5 cm) into a heavy saucepan or deep, heavy frying pan and heat to 325°F (165°C) on a deep-frying thermometer, or until a bit of rice dropped into the hot oil sizzles immediately on contact. Working in batches, fry the croquettes, turning as needed to color evenly, until they are a deep sunburned color and have a nice crisp crust, 5–7 minutes. Using a slotted spoon, transfer to paper towels to drain. Transfer to the platter in the oven to keep warm while you fry the remaining croquettes.

5 Serve the croquettes while the mozzarella core is still hot. They may be eaten with a knife and fork, but for the traditional telephone-cord effect, they should be grasped with a paper napkin and eaten out of hand.

In Roman pizzerias, a light Castelli Romani is the typical partner, but an oaky Chardonnay from Friuli or elsewhere would be a good alternative.

FOR THE TOMATO MIXTURE

1½ oz (15 g) dried porcini (cep) mushrooms

1 tablespoon extra-virgin olive oil

¼ lb (125 g) lean ground (minced) beef

1 small yellow onion, finely chopped

1 can (14 oz/440 g) tomato purée

Salt

FOR THE RICE

Salt

2 cups (14 oz/440 g) Arborio rice

2 large eggs, lightly beaten

2 tablespoons unsalted butter

2 tablespoons grated Parmigiano-Reggiano cheese

1 large egg

1 cup (4 oz/125 g) fine dried bread crumbs

½ lb (250 g) fresh mozzarella cheese, cut into rectangles the size and shape of large sugar cubes (about 24 pieces)

Olive oil, preferably extra-virgin, for deep-frying

Makes about 24 croquettes

ZUCCHINE A SCAPECE

Marinated Zucchini Slices

These simple marinated zucchini slices, flavored with a hint of mint, are constants of the antipasto buffets in Rome's trattorias. The word scapece *may derive from the Spanish* escabeche *(pickling), a technique it resembles. Any zucchini will do for this dish, but the best are the beautiful* zucchine romanesche, *which have light green skin and ridges that make lovely starlike slices when cut crosswise. They also contain relatively little water. Other zucchini will benefit from being cut several hours before frying and left to dry at room temperature on wire racks or kitchen towels to rid them of their extra water.*

2 cloves garlic

About ⅔ cup (5 fl oz/160 ml) extra-virgin olive oil

1 lb (500 g) small or medium-sized, firm zucchini (courgettes), trimmed and sliced ¼ inch (6 mm) thick

¼ teaspoon salt

1½–2 tablespoons red wine vinegar

About 10 fresh mint leaves, torn into pieces

Makes 4 small servings

1 Halve the garlic cloves lengthwise, cut away any green shoots, and cut each half lengthwise into 2 or 3 pieces. Set aside.

2 Pour the olive oil into a frying pan; it should be about 1 inch (2.5 cm) deep. Place over medium-high heat and heat until a zucchini slice dropped into it sizzles on contact. Put a single layer of zucchini slices in the pan and cook, turning once, until well browned on both sides, about 5 minutes total, paying closer attention to the color than the clock. As the zucchini slices are ready, lift them out of the oil with a slotted spoon, give them a little shake, and put them in a small serving bowl. Continue adding the zuccini slices to the oil one batch at a time in order to maintain the temperature of the oil.

3 Sprinkle the zucchini lightly with salt, add the garlic, and stir in 1½ tablespoons vinegar, mixing well but gently. Add the mint leaves and stir once. Place in the refrigerator or in a cool place until the slices are no longer warm, about 30 minutes.

4 Taste and adjust with a little more vinegar, if desired. The zucchini slices are delicate and delicious eaten right away, but, if you prefer them tarter, wait until the next day, after they have had a chance to marinate. Serve them straight from the bowl.

Emphasize the southern character of the dish with a Campanian white wine, such as Fiano di Avellino or Greco di Tufo.

FIORI DI ZUCCA FRITTI IN PASTELLA

Fried Squash Blossoms with Mozzarella and Anchovies

Fiori di zucca, or "squash blossoms," are the male flowers of the zucchini. The female flowers, which often remain attached to the zucchini sold in Roman markets, lack the distinguishing long stems. The male flower is preferable here, but is often hard to find outside Italy. These bright orange blooms can be deep-fried, as in this dish, or added to delicate pasta sauces, risottos, or frittatas. Like many traditional Roman fried foods, this recipe, which calls for dipping the flowers in the simple batter known as pastella before slipping them into hot oil, originated in the Ghetto, but today is prepared throughout the city.

1 Cut off the stem of each flower, remove the sharp, protruding points of the calyx at its base, and then remove the pistils from inside, trying not to tear the flower. Rinse the flowers and dry gently with a kitchen towel or paper towels.

2 Place 1 piece of anchovy and 1 piece of cheese in the cavity of each flower and press the petals closed. If any flower is torn, just wrap its petals around the filling. (When fried, the batter will help hold the package together.) Gently lay the stuffed flowers in a single layer on a plate.

3 Sift 2 cups (10 oz/315 g) of the flour into a bowl. Add 1¼ cups (10 fl oz/310 ml) water and mix with a fork until a thick batter forms. To test, dip your finger into the batter; it should coat it without dripping. Adjust the consistency by adding more flour or more water. Stir in ¼ teaspoon salt and the vinegar. Put the remaining 1 cup (5 oz/155 g) flour in a bowl.

4 Preheat the oven to 150°F (65°C) and put an ovenproof platter in it. Pour olive oil to a depth of 2 inches (2.5 cm) into a heavy saucepan or deep, heavy frying pan and heat to 325°F (165°C) on a deep-frying thermometer, or until a bit of batter dropped into the hot oil sizzles immediately on contact. Holding 1 stuffed flower by its base, dip it first into the flour, coating evenly and shaking off the excess, and then into the batter, coating generously. Lay the flower gently in the oil. Repeat, adding 2 or 3 more flowers and being careful not to crowd the pan. Deep-fry until golden brown on all sides, about 5 minutes total, paying more attention to the color than to the clock. Using a slotted spoon or tongs, transfer the flowers to paper towels to drain. Transfer to the platter in the oven to keep warm. Repeat with the remaining stuffed flowers.

5 Sprinkle the fried flowers lightly with salt and then arrange on a warmed platter or individual plates. Serve at once.

Serve with a Castelli Romani white wine, such as Frascati or Marino, or emphasize the floral accents with a Gewürztraminer from Alto Adige.

12 zucchini (courgette) flowers

4 olive oil–packed anchovy fillets, each cut into 3 pieces

¼ lb (125 g) fresh mozzarella or *mozzarella di bufala* (page 105), cut into 12 pieces

3 cups (15 oz/470 g) all-purpose (plain) flour, plus more if needed

Salt

½ teaspoon white wine vinegar

Olive oil, preferably extra-virgin, for deep-frying

Makes 4 servings

INSALATA DI FINOCCHIO

Fennel, Orange, and Olive Salad

According to Greek mythology, Prometheus stole fire from the gods on Mount Olympus and carried it to earth in a fennel stalk. The aromatic bulb has been a key player in Mediterranean cookery ever since. Fennel is a favorite winter vegetable in Rome, cooked or raw, but the addition of orange, recognized throughout Italy as fennel's natural partner, is of Sicilian origin. The small brown-purple olives named for Gaeta, a picturesque port town in southern Lazio, are favorites in the capital for cooking and eating. This refreshing salad can go at either end of the meal, as an antipasto or a contorno.

2 rounded, rather than flat, fennel bulbs

1 blood orange or flavorful regular orange

Salt and white pepper

2 tablespoons extra-virgin olive oil

About 24 Gaeta olives or other flavorful brine-cured black olives, pitted

Makes 4 servings

1 Trim off the stalks and fronds from the fennel bulbs and reserve for another use or discard. Remove the outer layer from the bulbs and cut away the tough core. Using a sharp knife, cut the bulbs lengthwise into slices about ⅛ inch (3 mm) thick.

2 Using a sharp knife, cut a slice off both ends of the orange to reveal the flesh. Place the orange upright on the cutting board and, using the knife, cut downward to remove the peel and pith, following the contour of the fruit. Cut the orange in half through the stem end, then slice each half crosswise as thinly as possible. Eliminate any seeds and visible pith.

3 Salt causes fennel to throw off water, and for many people the olives provide sufficient saltiness for this salad. But if you want to be able to add salt to the salad, a few minutes in advance of serving, place the fennel slices in a colander, sprinkle them with salt, and let stand to drain off any water before proceeding.

4 Divide the fennel slices among 4 plates. Lay the orange slices on top of the fennel, again dividing evenly, and drizzle the olive oil evenly over the top. Season with salt, if desired, and white pepper, and scatter about 6 olives on each plate. Let stand for a few minutes before serving, to give the orange slices time to release some of their juice onto the fennel layer.

Serve with a dry white wine such as Pinot Grigio.

BRESAOLA CON RUGHETTA E SCAGLIE DI PARMIGIANO

Cured Beef with Arugula and Parmigiano-Reggiano

Usually associated with the far north of Italy, bresaola, air-dried cured beef, is a fixture of the Roman Jewish table as a substitute for prosciutto and is popular today for its low fat content. Arugula, which Italians call rucola *and Romans call* rughetta *(or* ruchetta coltivata*), shares the stage with* rughetta selvatica *(page 45). Either will do in this recipe. Finally, Parmigiano-Reggiano, an "import" from the Emilia-Romagna region, is as well rooted in Rome as elsewhere in Italy. This popular antipasto also makes a fine summer main dish.*

1 Tear the arugula leaves into a bowl, sprinkle with salt, and dress with the 2 teaspoons olive oil. Toss to mix well. Add a grinding of pepper if the arugula is mild; often its own peppery taste is sufficient.

2 Choose a white or light-colored serving plate or individual plates that highlight the colors of the ingredients. Arrange the slices of *bresaola* around the edge of the platter or plates. Place the arugula in the middle. Using a handheld cheese slicer or a vegetable peeler, shave the cheese over the arugula.

3 Sprinkle lightly with salt and freshly ground pepper, and serve at once. Place the olive oil bottle on the table for diners to add to the *bresaola*. Pass the lemon wedges for squeezing over the top.

Serve with a sparkling wine such as a *metodo classico* or a sparkling Frascati.

2 cups (2 oz/60 g) arugula (rocket) leaves, tough stems removed, leaves rinsed and dried

Salt and freshly ground pepper

2 teaspoons extra-virgin olive oil, plus more for serving

16 paper-thin slices *bresaola,* about 4½ oz (140 g) total weight

About 1½-oz (45-g) wedge Parmigiano-Reggiano cheese

4 lemon wedges

Makes 4 servings

How to Choose Olive Oil

A careful reading of the label is the first step to selecting a superior oil. The finest oils include a guarantee of provenance in the form of a *denominazione d'origine protetta* (DOP) or, more rarely, an *indicazione geografica protetta* (IGP), official quality designations that guarantee the origin of food products and agricultural products, respectively. To gain these highly respected stamps of excellence, producers within a geographical zone must meet the area's rigorous standards.

Top-quality extra-virgin olive oils—the expensive estate-bottled kind that come in small, dark bottles with detailed information about growing and production conditions—should be used raw as a condiment. For sautéing and frying, use a good but less expensive extra-virgin oil.

Although much of the extra-virgin oil found in Roman kitchens comes from nearby Tuscany and Umbria, Lazio boasts two excellent DOP oils. Sabina DOP is produced in the Sabine Hills, in the provinces of Rieti and Rome, home to Europe's oldest producing olive trees. The other is fragrant, fruity Canino DOP, from the province of Viterbo.

FRITTATA DI ASPARAGI

Asparagus Frittata

The Italian frittata differs from the French omelet in that the latter is folded, with filling at the center, while the former is flat, with the filling distributed evenly throughout. Some Romans like their frittata to be as thick as a quiche, while most others prefer it thin enough to slip between two slices of bread for a sandwich. This recipe yields a fairly thin frittata, but once you master turning it, you can try varying the amount of eggs to find the thickness you like best. Here, the filling uses the distinctive spring flavor of fresh asparagus. Other favorite fillings include zucchini (courgettes), leeks, or artichoke hearts.

1 lb (500 g) asparagus

2 tablespoons extra-virgin olive oil, plus more as needed

4 large eggs, at room temperature

3 tablespoons grated Parmigiano-Reggiano cheese

Salt and freshly ground pepper

Makes 4 servings

1 Snap or trim off the tough end of each asparagus spear. Cut off the tips and set aside. Then, if the skin seems tough, peel the bottom one-third or so of each spear with a vegetable peeler or paring knife. Cut the spears on the diagonal into slices about ½ inch (12 mm) thick. If the tips are more than 1 inch (2.5 cm) long, cut them in half on the diagonal.

2 In a 10-inch (25-cm) nonstick frying pan over medium heat, warm 1 tablespoon of the olive oil. Add the asparagus slices, but not the tips, and sauté for about 2 minutes. Add 1 tablespoon water, reduce the heat to low, cover, and cook until the asparagus slices are very tender. This will take a few minutes. Using a slotted spoon, transfer the asparagus to a small bowl and set aside.

3 Return the pan to medium heat and add the remaining 1 tablespoon of the olive oil. Add the asparagus tips and cook, stirring, until tender, about 5 minutes. If the pan seems dry, add a little more olive oil, then return the cooked slices and toss all of the asparagus pieces together for a few seconds. Reduce the heat to low and add a quick swirl of olive oil. Using a wooden spoon, spread the asparagus pieces evenly over the bottom of the pan.

4 In a small bowl, whisk the eggs until blended. Stir in the cheese. Add ¼ teaspoon salt and a few grinds of pepper and stir to mix.

5 Raise the heat under the asparagus to medium-low and pour in the egg mixture, being careful not to dislodge the asparagus. Cook gently, without poking or prodding, until the egg mixture has set, about 15 minutes. If you are worried that the frittata may be sticking, once the edge has set, lift the edge with a plastic or wooden spatula to make sure the frittata moves freely. When the frittata has set and comes free from the pan, slide it carefully onto a flat dinner plate. Set the plate on one outstretched hand and invert the empty pan over it. Invert the pan and the plate together so that the frittata drops back into the pan, with the unbrowned side on the bottom. Remove the plate and return the pan briefly to medium-low heat to brown the second side.

6 Slide the frittata onto a serving plate. Cut into wedges and serve warm or at room temperature.

Serve with a crisp white wine, such as a Sauvignon Blanc, from Lazio or elsewhere.

INSALATA DI MARE

Seafood Salad

The term insalata di mare *covers a broad range of dishes in Rome, from the standard trattoria jumble of squid rings and shrimp to delicate compositions that change according to a chef's whim or the day's catch. This salad, inspired by a recipe from Al Presidente, one of Rome's premier fish restaurants, uses prized ingredients briefly cooked and laid gently on a bed of greens. It is lightly dressed to preserve the flavor of each element. If you have a bottle of prized aged balsamic vinegar on the shelf, add just a few drops at the end.*

1 If using shrimp or langoustines, peel or cut away their body shells but leave their heads and tails intact. With a small, sharp knife, cut a shallow groove along the back and lift out and discard the dark vein. If using scallops, leave them whole. Pour water to a depth of about 2 inches (5 cm) into the bottom of a steamer and bring to a boil. Arrange the shrimp, langoustines, and scallops on the steamer rack, cover, and steam until the crustaceans turn pink and the scallops are just opaque throughout, about 5 minutes. Remove from the steamer and set aside while you finish cooking the remaining seafood.

2 If using cuttlefish, squid, or octopus, cut into bite-sized pieces, or leave whole if small. Bring a saucepan three-fourths full of water to a boil over high heat. Squeeze a few drops of lemon juice over the shellfish. Boil just until tender, 2–3 minutes. Drain and set aside.

3 Arrange a bed of greens on individual plates or a single large platter. Sprinkle lightly with salt and drizzle with a little of the olive oil. Arrange the seafood on the greens and garnish with 1 or 2 citrus slices for each serving. Drizzle lightly with the remaining olive oil. If using the balsamic vinegar, place just 1 drop on each of the white seafood pieces. Mix together the chives and parsley and sprinkle lightly on top. Serve at once.

Serve with a fruity white wine such as Greco di Tufo.

1 lb (500 g) mixed shellfish such as shrimp (prawns) in the shell, langoustines, sea scallops, cleaned small cuttlefish, cleaned squid, and cleaned whole small octopus or octopus pieces, in any combination

½ lemon or lime

3 cups (3 oz/90 g) mâche leaves or other mild salad greens

Salt

About 4 tablespoons (2 fl oz/ 60 ml) finest extra-virgin olive oil

FOR THE GARNISH

Lemon, lime, or orange slices, or a combination

Best-quality balsamic vinegar (optional)

Minced fresh chives and flat-leaf (Italian) parsley for garnish

Makes 4 servings

Fish and Shellfish

Long before Catholicism brought meatless Fridays, Romans regularly sat down to fresh and preserved fish. Gourmets of the first century BC introduced fish farming, and during the empire, fish were imported from the Black Sea.

In later centuries, Rome principally looked to the Tiber and the Tyrrhenian for its fish and shellfish, and some local waters still provide many of the city's favorites. Calamari or *totani* (squid) and *polpo* (octopus), in various sizes, are popular, as are *scampi* (langoustines), *gamberi* (shrimp), *cozze* (mussels), and *vongole* (clams). Cooks turn to *orata* (gilthead bream) and *spigola* (sea bass), often farmed, as well as *rombo* (turbot) for simple white fish dishes. *Razza* (skate), known as *arzilla* in Rome, holds an honored place in the local cooking, as do dark-fleshed fish, such as *sgombro* (mackerel) and fresh *alici* (anchovies).

Restaurants near the volcanic lakes to the north and south of Rome serve freshwater fish such as *persico* (perch). In the past, the Tiber yielded salmon, sturgeon, and small eels, but nowadays only herons and cormorants fish for their dinner there.

LA TIELLA DI GAETA CON LE CIPOLLE

Onion and Herb Tart

Tiella is a southern Italian word for a baking pan and, by extension, its contents, often a savory pie or tart. The town of Gaeta, near the border of Campania, has earned recognition for its tiella, a particular kind of torta salata (savory tart). Once a whole meal for the poor, today such dishes are fixtures of antipasto buffets. The tiella di Gaeta comes in many forms, with, among other fillings, anchovies and tomatoes, escarole and salt cod, or, as here, onions and scamorza cheese. This recipe calls for a 12-inch (30-cm) cake pan, but the size and shape of the pan for this rustic dish is not crucial.

FOR THE PASTRY

½ cake (⅔ oz/10 g) fresh yeast or 1¼ teaspoons active dry yeast

2 cups (10 oz/315 g) all-purpose (plain) flour

2 cups (10 oz/315 g) semolina flour

½ teaspoon salt

2 tablespoons extra-virgin olive oil

FOR THE FILLING

3 tablespoons extra-virgin olive oil, plus more for brushing

4 large white onions, thinly sliced (about 3 cups/12 oz/375 g)

Salt and freshly ground pepper

1 cup (8 oz/250 g) ricotta cheese, preferably fresh

6 oz (185 g) smoked *scamorza* or other mild smoked cheese such as Gouda, shredded

1 tablespoon *each* minced fresh flat-leaf (Italian) parsley, marjoram, thyme, and sage

3 large eggs

Makes one 12-inch (30-cm) tart, or 8 servings

1 To make the crust, in a small bowl, stir the yeast into 2 tablespoons lukewarm water. Let stand until creamy, about 3 minutes.

2 On a large work surface, sift together the flours and salt into a mound, then make a well in the center. Pour the yeast mixture, olive oil, and ¼ cup (2 fl oz/60 ml) lukewarm water into the well. Using the fingers of one hand, swirl the liquid in a circular motion, gradually incorporating flour from the sides of the well. Slowly add 1 cup (8 fl oz/250 ml) water to the well at the same time, and mix until all the ingredients are well combined and a rough dough has formed. Knead vigorously, stretching and pressing and striking the dough against the work surface until it is soft and smooth and comes away cleanly from your hands and the work surface, about 10 minutes. To check if the dough is sufficiently kneaded, cut off a piece. The cut surface should be pocked with small air holes.

3 Shape the dough into a ball. Lightly flour a large bowl, place the dough in it, cover with a damp kitchen towel, and let stand in a warm place until the dough has doubled in volume, about 1 hour.

4 Meanwhile, make the filling: In a large frying pan over medium heat, warm 2 tablespoons of the olive oil. Add the onions and sauté slowly, seasoning with a little salt and pepper. When the onions are just starting to brown, after about 8 minutes, remove the pan from the heat.

5 If using fresh ricotta, drain as described in step 1 on page 169. In a bowl, combine the ricotta and

scamorza cheeses and add the herbs, a pinch of salt, and a few grinds of pepper. Then beat in the eggs one at a time, mixing well with a wooden spoon after each addition until fully incorporated. Add the onions and their oil to the cheese mixture and mix well.

6 Preheat the oven to 375°F (190°C). Have ready a 12-inch (30-cm) round cake pan with 2-inch (5-cm) sides (or any large metal baking sheet). Oil the pan with olive oil, even if it is nonstick.

7 Punch down the dough and turn it out onto a lightly floured work surface. Divide the dough into 2 pieces, one slightly larger than the other. Using a rolling pin or your fingers, stretch and press the larger piece into a round about 16 inches (40 cm) in diameter and ⅟₁₆ inch (2 mm) thick. Transfer the round to the pan, and press it into the bottom and up the sides, leaving at least a 1–2-inch (2.5–5-cm) overhang. Fill with the onion-cheese mixture, spreading it evenly, and drizzle with the remaining 1 tablespoon olive oil. Roll out the remaining dough into a 12-inch (30-cm) round about ⅟₁₆ inch thick. Carefully lay it over the filling and trim to size with no overhang. Bring the overhang of the lower crust up over the edges of the top crust, and press against the top.

8 Prick the top in several places with a fork and brush lightly with olive oil. Bake until golden brown and quite firm, 40–45 minutes. Transfer to a rack and let cool. Serve at room temperature, cut into wedges.

Gaeta is near the border of Campania, so a Campanian white wine such as Fiano di Avellino is a good match.

PRIMI

A handful of greens, a few clams, or a sprinkling of cheese and pepper

and a toss in the pan turn plain pasta into a Roman *primo piatto.*

The first course in Rome is usually pasta, to which most Romans are addicted. Gnocchi and thick soups like *pasta e ceci* share the honored status. A day that does not include a meal with a proper *primo* is starvation. The traditional repertory, extending from the simplest sauce of cracked pepper and pecorino romano to the most labor-intensive ravioli, covers every taste and ingredient. A trattoria will almost always offer the popular local dishes—*pasta alla gricia, al pomodoro,* and *al ragù*—while in more sophisticated restaurants, the *primo* is a canvas for the chef's imagination.

PASTA E CECI

Pasta and Chickpea Soup

The combination of pasta and legumes is a Roman perennial. Borlotti beans, lentils, and chickpeas mix and match happily with ditalini (thimbles), maltagliati (egg pasta scraps), quadrucci (pasta squares), or, as in this recipe, taglierini (long flat noodles), broken into pieces. This dish became a Roman icon with the 1958 comic film I soliti ignoti *(Big Deal on Madonna Street). In it, bungling burglars break through a wall, not to a pawn shop, as they expect, but to a kitchen, where they console themselves with a pot of* pasta e ceci. *This recipe is based on the version served at Ristorante Paris, in the heart of Trastevere.*

1   Pick over the chickpeas, discarding any grit or misshapen beans. Rinse well, place in a large bowl or pot, and add the baking soda, 1 tablespoon salt, and warm water to cover generously. Cover and place in the refrigerator overnight.

2   Drain the chickpeas and return them to the pot. Add cold water to cover generously, 2 teaspoons salt, and 2 of the garlic cloves and bring to a boil over medium-high heat. Reduce the heat to medium-low (making sure to maintain a gentle simmer) and cook, uncovered, until tender, at least 1–2 hours; the timing will depend on the age of the chickpeas. Remove from the heat and drain, reserving the cooking water; you should have at least 2 cups (16 fl oz/500 ml) water.

3   While the chickpeas are cooking, in a small frying pan over medium heat, warm the ½ cup olive oil. Add the remaining 4 garlic cloves and the rosemary and fry until the garlic is golden brown, about 2 minutes. Pour the oil through a fine-mesh sieve held over a soup pot, and discard the garlic and rosemary. Add the tomatoes and their juice, the potatoes, 2 teaspoons salt, a few grinds of pepper, and the chile, and place over low heat. Cook slowly until the potatoes are soft, about 15 minutes.

4   Using a slotted spoon, transfer the potatoes to a bowl and mash with a fork. Return the potatoes to the pot over low heat, add the drained chickpeas and about 1 cup (8 fl oz/250 ml) of the cooking water (or lightly salted tap water), and cook for about 30 minutes to blend the flavors. (The soup can be made up to this point, covered, and refrigerated for up to 2 days.)

5   If the soup is very dense, add more of the chickpea cooking water or some lightly salted water to thin it to a good consistency. Then taste and adjust the seasoning with salt.

6   Meanwhile, bring a pot three-fourths full of water to a boil; add 1 tablespoon salt and the pasta and cook until still very al dente. Drain the pasta and add it to the soup. Cook, stirring to mix all the ingredients together, for 1–2 minutes longer.

7   Ladle the soup into a warmed tureen or shallow rimmed bowls, sprinkle with the parsley, and serve at once. Pass the pepper mill and olive oil at the table.

Serve with an interesting Lazio blend such as Concento, made of Shiraz and Cesanese.

2¼ cups (1 lb/500 g) dried chickpeas (garbanzo beans)

1 tablespoon baking soda (bicarbonate of soda)

Salt and freshly ground pepper

6 cloves garlic, crushed

½ cup (4 fl oz/125 ml) extra-virgin olive oil, plus more for serving

2 tablespoons chopped fresh rosemary

1 can (14 oz/440 g) plum (Roma) tomatoes

2 boiling potatoes, peeled and cut lengthwise into narrow wedges

1 small dried red chile

½ lb (250 g) *taglierini,* broken into 2-inch (5-cm) pieces

1 tablespoon minced fresh flat-leaf (Italian) parsley

Makes 4 servings

LA VIGNAROLA
Stewed Spring Vegetables

In springtime, la vignarola *is a veritable cult food, when, for a few magic weeks, young, tender fava beans, sweet shelling peas, and locally grown globe artichokes are available simultaneously in the markets. Many Romans insist that the ingredients be cooked together, while others maintain the vegetables must keep their separate identities until near the end, as in this version. Some feel that favas without* guanciale *is sacrilege; others tout the vegetarian version. Yet all agree that* la vignarola *fits in nearly anywhere in the meal, as a* primo, *a light main course, or a* contorno.

3 artichokes

2 lb (1 kg) young, tender fava (broad) beans in the pod

2 lb (1 kg) young, tender English peas in the pod

2 oz (60 g) *guanciale* (page 101), pancetta, or prosciutto, cut into small strips (optional)

1 or 2 tablespoons extra-virgin olive oil, plus more for serving

4 green (spring) onions, including pale tops, thinly sliced

Salt and freshly ground pepper

Makes 4–6 servings

1 Prepare the artichokes as directed for Braised Whole Artichokes (page 159), omitting the garlic. Set aside. Shell the fava beans and peas and set them aside in separate bowls. If using larger, older fava beans, bring a pot three-fourths full of water to a boil. Add the fava beans and blanch for 20 seconds. Drain and let cool. Split open the skin of each bean along its edge and slip the bean from the skin. Discard the skins. If using small, new favas, leave the skins on.

2 If using *guanciale,* place in a pan over medium heat and cook, stirring occasionally, until it starts to brown and render some of its fat, 2–3 minutes. If using pancetta or prosciutto, warm 1 tablespoon of the olive oil in the saucepan over medium heat, then add the pancetta or prosciutto and cook as described for *guanciale.* Add half of the green onions and cook, stirring, until translucent, about 10 minutes. Add the fava beans, stir a couple of times, and add about ½ cup (4 fl oz/125 ml) water, a pinch of salt, and a grind of pepper. Bring to a boil, reduce the heat to low, cover, and cook until the beans are just tender, about 20 minutes; the timing will depend on their size and age. Check the water level occasionally and add more as needed to keep a little liquid in the pan.

3 Meanwhile, in another saucepan over medium-low heat, warm 1 tablespoon olive oil. Add the remaining green onions and sauté until translucent, about 10 minutes. Stir in the peas, and add about ½ cup (4 fl oz/125 ml) water, a pinch of salt, and a grind of pepper. Bring to a boil, reduce the heat to low, cover, and cook until the peas are just tender, about 15 minutes; the timing will depend on their size and age. Be careful not to overcook the peas to the point where they lose their lovely green color.

4 When both the favas and the peas are cooked, combine them and their cooking liquid in a single saucepan and set aside.

5 Cut the braised artichokes in half lengthwise, then cut each half into 4 or 6 wedges and scrape away any sharp leaves or choke in the center of each wedge. Chop the wedges coarsely and add them to the peas and favas.

6 Place the saucepan over low heat, cover, and simmer until the vegetables are heated through, 10–15 minutes. Uncover, drizzle with a little olive oil, and then transfer to a warmed serving bowl or individual plates and serve at once. Or, if you can wait, the vegetables are even better reheated the next day.

Serve with a white wine with good structure and some oak, such as Cervaro della Sala from Umbria.

CREMA DI ZUCCA CON GAMBERETTI

Winter Squash Soup with Shrimp

Winter squashes are typically associated with northern Italy, where they are featured in risottos and tortelli di zucca *(stuffed pasta). But a handful of pumpkin and winter squash varieties, such as the richly flavored, dark green Marina di Chioggia, are sold at the vegetable markets of Rome and have always played a quiet but consistent role in the traditional cuisine. This modern take on an old-fashioned recipe is based on the version served at the elegant and creative restaurant Agata e Romeo in the Esquilino district.*

1 In a saucepan over low heat, warm together the olive oil and shallots and cook, stirring occasionally, until the shallots are translucent, about 10 minutes. Add the squash, potato, bay leaf, a generous pinch of salt, a couple grinds of white pepper, and about 3 cups (24 fl oz/750 ml) water, or as needed to cover. Raise the heat to medium-high, bring to a steady simmer, and cook, stirring occasionally, until the squash is very soft, about 30 minutes.

2 Remove and discard the bay leaf and let the soup cool slightly. In a blender or food processor, process the soup, working in batches if necessary, until a smooth purée forms. Return to the pan and reheat gently to serving temperature. Alternatively, purée in the pan with an immersion blender. Taste and adjust the seasoning with salt.

3 To make the garnish, in a small frying pan over medium heat, warm the olive oil. When it is hot, add the shrimp and sauté quickly just until they turn pink and are opaque throughout, about 2 minutes. Season with a pinch of salt and the dill.

4 Ladle the soup into warmed soup plates. Garnish each plate with shrimp. Serve at once.

Romeo Caraccio at Agata e Romeo recommends serving this soup with a fine, full-bodied Chardonnay from Lazio or elsewhere.

1 tablespoon extra-virgin olive oil

2 shallots, thinly sliced

1 lb (500 g) winter squash, such as butternut, acorn, or Hubbard, or pumpkin, such as Sugar Pie or Cheese, peeled and cut into 1-inch (2.5-cm) dice (about 3½ cups/ 12 oz/375 g)

1 medium boiling potato, peeled and cut into ½-inch (12-mm) dice (about ½ cup/2½ oz/75g)

1 bay leaf

Salt and freshly ground white pepper

FOR THE GARNISH

1 tablespoon extra-virgin olive oil

12 small shrimp (prawns), about ⅓ lb (170 g) total weight, peeled and deveined

Salt

1 teaspoon chopped fresh dill or wild fennel

Makes 4 servings

Fountains and Water

Rome's most prized and characteristic urban amenity is its fountains—sculpted magnificently and as big as a building, like the Trevi Fountain, or cast iron and as small as a fire hydrant, like the many street-corner *fontanelle* (little fountains). Since antiquity, Rome has prided itself on its water. Unless it is marked "*non potabile,*" it's all drinkable and can be a lifesaver on a hot day.

The sophisticated ancient Roman system of aqueducts and fountains ran dry during the Middle Ages but was revived in the Renaissance. Today, the local water infuses everything with wholesome goodness, from the coffee served at the neighborhood bars to most soups, which, like this one, often rely on water rather than stock.

For those who insist on *acqua minerale,* several locally bottled options are available. For centuries, the most famous local mineral water has been Fiuggi, from the mountains east of Rome. It is widely credited with dissolving kidney stones, including those of Michelangelo. Of the waters from springs along the Via Appia, the lightly fizzy Egeria is the most popular.

SPAGHETTI ALLA CARBONARA

Spaghetti with Eggs, Cured Pork, and Cheese

Dispute over the origin of this decidedly Roman dish never ends. Did the carbonari *(charcoal makers) invent it? Or was it American GIs looking for a way to use their bacon and egg rations? Or does the name describe the black, carbonlike flecks of pepper? Whatever the origin of this delicious dish, the key is the technique. Finding the precise point when the eggs, added raw to cooked spaghetti, are no longer liquid, but not yet fully cooked, makes this dish work.* Carbonara *lends itself to variation, too, with red pepper flakes instead of black pepper, wild asparagus instead of cured pork, or a grating of white truffle from Alba.*

6 oz (185 g) *guanciale* (page 101), pancetta, or bacon, preferably in a single piece or in slices at least ¼ inch (6 mm) thick

1 tablespoon extra-virgin olive oil (optional)

Salt and freshly ground pepper

1 lb (500 g) spaghetti

¼ cup (1 oz/30 g) grated *pecorino romano* cheese

¼ cup (1 oz/30 g) grated Parmigiano-Reggiano cheese, plus more as needed

2 large eggs plus 1 large egg yolk, at room temperature

Makes 4–6 servings

1 If using *guanciale* or pancetta, cut it into strips about ¾ inch (2 cm) long by ¼ inch (6 mm) thick. If using commercially sliced bacon, which will be thinner than ¼ inch, cut it into 1-inch (2.5-cm) pieces.

2 In a large frying pan over medium-low heat, combine the *guanciale* or other meat and olive oil and heat slowly until much of the fat is rendered and the meat has browned a little, about 15 minutes. It should take on an appealing color without becoming too crisp. Leave the meat and fat in the pan and cover to keep warm.

3 Bring a large pot three-fourths full of water (at least 4 qt/4 l) to a rapid boil over high heat. Add 1 tablespoon salt and the pasta and stir for the first minute of cooking and occasionally thereafter. Cook until al dente, according to the package instructions.

4 Meanwhile, in a bowl, mix together both of the cheeses. In another bowl, whisk together the whole eggs and egg yolk until well blended. Stir half the cheese mixture and several grinds of pepper into the eggs.

5 From this point on, timing and temperature are crucial. Put a large serving bowl in the sink and set a colander in the serving bowl. When the pasta is ready, pour it into the colander, so that its cooking water will warm the serving bowl. Grab the colander quickly out of the water and shake a couple of times. Toss the drained spaghetti into the pan with the *guanciale* and stir a couple of times to coat the pasta with the fat. Being careful not to burn your fingers, empty the hot water from the serving bowl, reserving 1 cup (8 fl oz/250 ml) in a separate small bowl or measuring pitcher. Transfer the pasta to the warmed bowl and, using a wooden spoon, stir the egg mixture into the pasta, mixing vigorously to coat the pasta evenly. Add a splash of the reserved cooking water if the pasta seems a little dry. Add an extra handful of grated Parmigiano-Reggiano cheese if it seems too wet. If the eggs scramble, the bowl or the pasta was too hot. If the eggs are too runny, something was too cold. If the beaten eggs were at room temperature to start, the bowl warmed with hot water should provide just enough heat.

6 Divide the pasta among warmed bowls and serve at once. Pass the remaining cheese at the table.

One regional classic deserves another: serve with a crisp, full-bodied white wine such as Frascati Superiore or Marino DOC.

RIGATONI CON GUANCIALE E CIPOLLA

Rigatoni with Guanciale and Onion

The Roman specialty spaghetti all'amatriciana, *with a simple sauce of* guanciale *or* pancetta, tomatoes, *and* pecorino romano, *has swept the globe in recent decades. Make the sauce in* bianco *(without tomatoes), and you have the original form of the dish, also known as* alla gricia. *Add a sweet red onion from the area of Tropea, in Calabria, and some green peppercorns and you have* cucina creativa—*in this case the inspiration of Angelo Troiani, co-owner (with his brothers) and chef of Ristorante Il Convivio, in the heart of old Rome.*

1 In a small frying pan over low heat, combine the onion, vinegar, olive oil, sugar, and a pinch of salt. Cook, stirring occasionally, until the onion wilts, about 5 minutes. Remove from the heat and set aside.

2 While the onion is cooking, in a large, deep frying pan over medium-low heat, fry the *guanciale* or pancetta until quite crisp, about 15 minutes. Remove the pan from the heat. Using a slotted spoon, remove half the *guanciale* pieces and set aside in a warm place. Add the cooked onion to the *guanciale* in the pan and keep warm over the lowest heat setting.

3 Bring a large pot three-fourths full of water (at least 4 qt/4 l) to a rapid boil over high heat. Add 1 tablespoon salt and the pasta and stir for the first minute of cooking and occasionally thereafter. Cook until al dente, according to the package instructions. Drain the pasta, but not too dry, and add to the pan holding the *guanciale* and onion. Remove the pan from the heat and toss the pasta to coat thoroughly. Add the cheese and toss again.

4 Transfer the pasta to a warmed serving bowl and sprinkle the reserved *guanciale* on top along with about 4 grinds of pepper. Alternatively, distribute the pasta among individual warmed plates and garnish each serving with a cluster of the reserved *guanciale* and a grind of pepper.

Serve with a full-bodied, tannic red such as a Chianti Classico or other Sangiovese-based wine.

1 sweet red onion, julienned

¼ cup (2 fl oz/60 ml) white wine vinegar

1 tablespoon extra-virgin olive oil

1 teaspoon sugar

Salt and freshly ground green or black peppercorns

½ lb (250 g) *guanciale* (right) or pancetta, cut into slices at least ¼ inch (6 mm) thick

1 lb (500 g) short pasta such as rigatoni or *mezzemaniche*

6 tablespoons (3 oz/90 g) grated *pecorino romano* cheese

Makes 4–6 servings

Guanciale, Pancetta, and Prosciutto

In Lazio's agrarian past, it was easier to glean fat from a pig than from olives, and peasants and city dwellers alike typically used lard, not oil, for frying and baking. The memory of those early tastes are evoked in the use of various types of salt-cured and air-cured pork in *spaghetti alla carbonara, all'amatriciana,* and *alla gricia,* among other dishes.

The word *guanciale* is used for any cheek meat, but in central Italy its first meaning is cured hog's jowl, favored by purists for its delicate, sweet flavor. Rubbed with salt and black or red pepper and aged for three months, the characteristic triangular cuts can be seen hanging in Rome's many *salumerie* (cured-meat shops). Pancetta (salt-cured bacon) is sold *arrotolata* (rolled) or *tesa* (in a slab). Some cooks prefer leaner, more strongly flavored pancetta to *guanciale,* especially for cooking with full-flavored ingredients such as tomatoes.

Prosciutto, air-cured ham, whether the prized sweet Parma and San Daniele varieties, or salty, rustic *prosciutto di montagna,* is also suitable for cooking, particularly if you prefer a leaner cut.

PASTA CON I BROCCOLI

Pasta with Broccolo Romanesco

In Rome, the word broccoli, *or its singular,* broccolo, *is used loosely for at least five different members of the Brassica family, all of which play major roles in the local diet throughout the colder months:* broccoli siciliani *(broccoli),* cavolfiore *(cauliflower),* cavolo broccolo *(a green cauliflower, which is properly called brocco-flower, but most people just describe it, rather than try to name it),* broccoletti *(broccoli rabe), and* broccolo romanesco, *a green cauliflower with pointed florets so new to the English-speaking world that it usually keeps its Italian name. This recipe calls for the last, but works equally well with any of them.*

1 large head *broccolo romanesco* or cauliflower, about 2 lb (1 kg), or 2 lb (1 kg) broccoli or broccoli rabe

Salt

2 tablespoons extra-virgin olive oil, plus more for serving

1 clove garlic, crushed

1 small dried red chile

6 olive oil–packed anchovy fillets

1 lb (500 g) penne, rigatoni, or *conchiglie*

Makes 4–6 servings

1 Discard only the largest or any discolored leaves from the vegetable. For *broccolo romanesco* or cauliflower, remove the core and separate the head into florets. For broccoli or broccoli rabe, separate the leaves and the florets. Cut off the bottom of the thinner, more tender stems and then cut into 1-inch (2.5-cm) pieces. Cut off the bottom of the thicker stems, and then use a vegetable peeler or paring knife to peel away the tough outer skin. Cut the thicker stems into ½-inch (12-mm) pieces.

2 Bring a large pot three-fourths full of water (at least 4 qt/4 l) to a rapid boil over high heat. Add 1 tablespoon salt and the *broccolo romanesco* or other vegetable and cook until quite tender, about 8 minutes.

3 Using a large slotted spoon or a wire skimmer, transfer the vegetable to a colander. Leave the water in the pot for cooking the pasta later.

4 In a large, deep frying pan over medium heat, warm the 2 tablespoons olive oil. Add the garlic and chile and cook, stirring occasionally, until the garlic is golden brown and the chile is browned, about 2 minutes (do not allow the garlic to burn). Using a slotted spoon, remove and discard the garlic and chile. Add the anchovies to the oil remaining in the pan and cook, pressing on them with a wooden spoon, until they dissolve into the oil. Add the boiled vegetable.

5 Meanwhile, bring the vegetable cooking water back to a rapid boil, add the pasta, and stir for the first minute of cooking and occasionally thereafter.

6 Sauté the vegetable gently while the pasta cooks, pushing it around and breaking up the pieces with a wooden spoon. When the pasta is about half done, stir a ladleful of the pasta water into the frying pan. Let the water evaporate, then stir in a second ladleful of water, again letting it evaporate.

7 Cook the pasta until al dente, according to the package instructions. Drain it, but not too dry, and reserve about 1 cup (8 fl oz/250 ml) of the cooking water. Add the pasta to the frying pan, remove from the heat, and toss together the pasta and vegetable until well combined. Add a bit of the reserved cooking water if the pasta seems too dry.

8 Transfer the pasta to a warmed serving bowl or individual bowls. Top with a swirl of olive oil and serve at once.

Serve with a fruity white wine such as Frascati Superiore.

CONCHIGLIE ALLA CAPRESE

Pasta Shells with Mozzarella, Tomatoes, and Basil

The taste of summer in Rome is the taste of tomatoes and basil, and a favorite dish of locals is insalata caprese, *layers of sliced tomatoes and mozzarella drizzled with olive oil and bedecked with fresh basil leaves. It was only a matter of time before this popular salad became a* primo piatto *in the form of this pasta dish. Because it can be prepared ahead of time and served at room temperature, it solves the perennial problem of* terrazzo *or garden entertaining: how to attend to the cooking indoors without ignoring your guests outdoors.*

1 If using cherry tomatoes, cut them in half through the stem end. If using larger tomatoes, cut them into pieces the size of a cherry tomato half. Put the cut tomatoes into a bowl and add the olive oil and one-third of the basil leaves. Set aside at room temperature to allow the flavors to blend while you prepare the remaining ingredients.

2 Cut the mozzarella into ¾-inch (2-cm) cubes, or coarsely shred it with your hands. Set aside.

3 Bring a large pot three-fourths full of water (at least 4 qt/4 l) to a rapid boil over high heat. Add 1 tablespoon salt and the pasta and stir for the first minute of cooking and occasionally thereafter. Cook until al dente, according to the package instructions.

4 Just before the pasta is done, add ½ teaspoon salt and a few grinds of black pepper to the tomatoes. When the pasta is ready, drain it, but not too dry, and put it into a serving bowl. Pour the tomato mixture over it, add the anchovies, capers, olives, and a sprinkle of red pepper flakes, if using, and mix well. Let the pasta cool for about 5 minutes, then stir in the mozzarella pieces. (The pasta should be cool enough so that the mozzarella does not melt.)

5 The pasta can be made up to 2 hours in advance and kept at room temperature, never refrigerated. Spoon into individual bowls or onto plates, or serve in a large bowl as part of a buffet.

Serve with a crisp white wine such as a Sauvignon Blanc.

---

1 lb (500 g) cherry or grape tomatoes or mixed heirloom tomatoes

½ cup (4 fl oz/125 ml) extra-virgin olive oil

About ½ cup (½ oz/15 g) fresh basil leaves, torn into pieces

½ lb (250 g) *mozzarella di bufala* (right)

Salt and freshly ground black pepper

1 lb (500 g) *conchiglie* or other short pasta

8 olive oil–packed anchovy fillets, coarsely chopped (optional)

1 tablespoon salt-packed capers, well rinsed (optional)

1 cup (5 oz/155 g) Gaeta or Kalamata olives, pitted, or 1 tablespoon black olive paste (optional)

Red pepper flakes (optional)

Makes 4–6 servings

Mozzarella di Bufala

Mozzarella di bufala is made by hand from the milk of the water buffalo. Each ball of smooth, white cheese weighs about a pound (500 g) and displays the characteristic scar where it was separated from the mass (*mozzare* means "to cut off"). The cheese is also sold in smaller balls and in *trecce* (braids). The flavor is pronounced and the soft but resistant texture sublime, and when the mozzarella is sliced, beads of milk ooze from pores in the cut surface.

Look for *mozzarella di bufala campana DOP.* Most of it is produced in Campania, but part of the official zone lies in southern Lazio. Similar cheeses made from cow's milk are properly called *fior di latte,* though they are often dubbed simply mozzarella or *mozzarella fresca.*

Romans use a great deal of mozzarella, primarily choosing the more abundant *fior di latte,* partly for economy and partly because it gives off less liquid when it melts. Both kinds turn up on pizza, in *insalata caprese,* and in the traditional snack *mozzarella in carrozza,* a fried mozzarella sandwich.

FUSILLI CON I CARCIOFI

Fusilli with Artichokes

Imagine a place where the chill of winter is alleviated by the most beautiful light the world has ever seen and by the arrival in the markets of so many artichokes that you have to think up new ways to use them. Such is Rome. For this recipe, size and shape are not important—in fact, this is a good chance to use up some of the less beautiful specimens. The artichokes should be tender, however, so trim them aggressively of any tough, inedible parts before cooking, and use as much pasta water as you need to make them soft and creamy. If you have any leftovers, use them to make a frittata.

1 lemon, halved

8 baby artichokes or 4 large artichokes

2 tablespoons extra-virgin olive oil, plus more for serving

1 clove garlic, crushed

Salt and freshly ground pepper

¼ cup (2 fl oz/60 ml) dry white wine or water

1 lb (500 g) fusilli, penne, *mezzemaniche,* or rigatoni

Makes 4–6 servings

1 Fill a bowl with water and squeeze the juice of the lemon into it. Working with 1 artichoke at a time, trim off the base of the stem, then peel away the stem's dark, tough, stringy outer layer. Remove all the tough outer leaves until you reach the pale, tender inner leaves. Holding a small, sharp knife in your dominant hand and the artichoke in your other hand, turn the artichoke against the blade, raising the knife with each turn, to carve a sphere. Artistic perfection is not very important, but removing all the tough parts is. Then cut off any tough tops of the remaining leaves until only the tender edible portion remains. Cut the artichokes in half lengthwise, then cut each half into wedges not more than ½ inch (12 mm) wide at the widest point. (If using baby artichokes, simply quarter them.) Scrape away the choke (the fibrous hairs surrounding the heart). As you finish trimming each artichoke, drop it in the bowl of lemon water to keep it from turning black.

2 In a large, deep frying pan over medium heat, warm the 2 tablespoons olive oil. Add the garlic and cook, stirring occasionally, until it is a deep golden brown, about 2 minutes. Using a slotted spoon, remove and discard the garlic.

3 Meanwhile, bring a pot three-fourths full of water (at least 4 qt/4 l) to a rapid boil over high heat.

4 While the water is heating, add the artichokes to the frying pan over medium-high heat, season with salt and pepper, and cook, stirring, until starting to brown and soften, about 10 minutes. Reduce the heat to very low, add the wine, cover, and cook the

artichokes, stirring occasionally, until they are quite tender, about 25 minutes.

5 When the artichokes are about half done, after about 15 minutes, add 1 tablespoon salt and the pasta to the boiling water and stir for the first minute of cooking and occasionally thereafter.

6 When the pasta is about half done, uncover the artichokes, stir a ladleful of the pasta water into the frying pan, let it evaporate, and then stir in a second ladleful and again let it evaporate. Continue to add the water and let it evaporate until the pasta is ready. At the same time, use a wooden spoon to break up the artichoke pieces. (If they are not tender enough to cut with a wooden spoon, add more pasta water and cover the pan until they soften.)

7 Cook the pasta until al dente, according to the package instructions. Drain it, but not too dry, add it to the frying pan, and remove from the heat. Toss together the pasta and artichokes until well combined.

8 Divide the pasta among warmed bowls, top each with a swirl of olive oil, and serve at once.

Serve with a soft, fruity red wine such as a Cabernet Sauvignon from Lazio or elsewhere.

TONNARELLI CACIO E PEPE

Tonnarelli with Pecorino and Pepper

Pasta, grated cheese, and black pepper—sounds simple. Yet few dishes in the Roman repertoire are trickier to get right. First, there are two schools, dry and wet. The former expects a grainy consistency, the latter a creamy sauce. In each case you need a sure hand and superb ingredients. Tonnarelli *are a kind of chewy, square-cut fresh spaghetti, typical of Roman cooking. The modern version is the direct descendant of* maccheroni alla chitarra, *pasta cut on a wire frame that recalls guitar strings. If you don't wish to make* tonnarelli *at home, use 1 pound (500 g) dried* spaghetti alla chitarra *or regular spaghetti.*

1 To make the pasta, mound the flour on a work surface and make a well in the center. Break the eggs into the well, and then add ½ teaspoon salt and the olive oil. Using a fork or your fingers, and working in a circular motion, gradually incorporate the flour into the eggs until a rough dough forms. Lightly flour the work surface as necessary and energetically knead the dough until it is smooth and elastic, at least 10 minutes. Shape into a ball, place in a bowl, cover the bowl with plastic wrap, and let the dough rest for at least 30 minutes or for up to 2 hours.

2 Divide the dough into 4 equal pieces. Flatten 1 piece slightly with your palm; re-cover the remaining 3 pieces. Set the rollers of a hand-cranked pasta machine at the widest setting and pass the dough through the rollers. Flour the dough lightly if it seems to be sticking, and pass it through the same setting 2 more times. Adjust the rollers to the next narrower setting. Fold the dough into thirds, as you would a letter, and pass it through the rollers. Repeat 1 or 2 times, again flouring as needed to prevent sticking. Fold and roll 2 or 3 times through each successively narrower setting, stopping at the third to the last setting. Lay the finished sheet on a lightly floured surface. Repeat with the remaining 3 pieces.

3 Cut the sheets into 12-inch (30-cm) lengths. Fit the machine with the narrowest cutter, and pass each sheet through the cutter, yielding narrow, square-cut ribbons. Place on lightly floured kitchen towels and dust lightly with flour to prevent sticking. Fluff them with your fingers frequently and cover with a kitchen towel until ready to cook.

4 Bring a large pot three-fourths full of water (at least 4 qt/4 l) to a rapid boil over high heat. While the water is heating, begin making the sauce. Place the peppercorns in a small frying pan over low heat and heat until fragrant, about 5 minutes. Remove from the heat, pour into a cloth napkin or a piece of waxed paper, and crush with a blunt instrument, such as a meat mallet. The resulting pepper should be considerably coarser than what a pepper mill produces.

5 When the water is boiling, add 1 tablespoon salt and the pasta and stir briefly to prevent sticking. Cook just until the pasta comes to the surface but is not quite done (1–2 minutes for fresh pasta). While the pasta is cooking, put a ladleful of the cooking water and the olive oil into a large, deep frying pan. Add a small handful of the cheese and mix vigorously with a fork or whisk. When the pasta is ready, using a spaghetti fork or a handheld colander, lift it from the water and add it to the frying pan. (If using a standard colander, reserve 1½ cups (12 fl oz/375 ml) water and add it to the pan with the pasta.)

6 Place the pan over low heat. Gradually add the remaining cheese, the crushed pepper, and spoonfuls of the pasta water as needed to make a creamy sauce. Toss to coat the pasta thoroughly, stirring and tossing for about 3 minutes. Serve at once in warmed bowls.

Serve with a light, young red wine such as Cesanese.

FOR THE PASTA

3 cups (15 oz/470 g) all-purpose (plain) flour

4 large eggs

Salt

1 teaspoon extra-virgin olive oil

FOR THE SAUCE

2 teaspoons peppercorns

Salt

1 tablespoon extra-virgin olive oil

1½ cups (6 oz/185 g) grated *pecorino romano* cheese

Makes 4–6 servings

SPAGHETTI ALLE VONGOLE VERACI

Spaghetti with Clams in Their Shells

In Rome, most "vongole veraci," characterized by variegated shells about 1½ inches (4 cm) wide and by two little "horns" (siphons), are actually farmed Japanese littleneck clams rather than the prized, and increasingly rare, native species. They are most commonly used in spaghetti alle vongole, *part of the pantheon of Roman pastas—carbonara, cacio e pepe, and* gricia *are others—whose sauces are created directly on the cooked pasta. That means the dish is easy to put together but hard to fake: timing, temperature, an experienced hand, and, especially, undivided attention make all the difference.*

2 lb (1 kg) littleneck or Manila clams in the shell, scrubbed

Salt

¼ cup (2 fl oz/60 ml) extra-virgin olive oil, plus more for finishing

2 cloves garlic, crushed

1 small dried red chile

1 lb (500 g) spaghetti

2 tablespoons minced fresh flat-leaf (Italian) parsley

Makes 4–6 servings

1 In a large bowl or the sink, soak the clams in salted water to cover for about 30 minutes. (Use this time to assemble what you will need for the recipe.) Discard any clams that rise to the surface, then drain, rinse well, and place in a large frying pan.

2 Bring a large pot three-fourths full of water (at least 4 qt/4 l) to a rapid boil over high heat.

3 In a second large, deep frying pan over medium heat, warm the ¼ cup olive oil. Add the garlic and chile and cook, stirring occasionally, until the garlic is golden brown, about 2 minutes. Remove the pan from the heat and, using a slotted spoon, remove and discard the garlic and chile. Set the pan with the oil aside.

4 When the pasta water is boiling, put the pan holding the clams over high heat and cover it. Add 1 tablespoon salt and the pasta to the water and stir for the first minute of cooking and occasionally thereafter.

5 After the pasta has cooked for 2 minutes, uncover the clams, reduce the heat to medium-high, and don't take your eyes off them. Cook the clams just until they open, only a couple of minutes. As they open, use tongs to transfer them in their shells to the pan holding the olive oil. Be careful not to bring any water with them, and discard any clams that did not open. When all the clams are in the second pan, strain the liquid in the first pan through a fine-mesh sieve lined with 2 or 3 layers of cheesecloth (muslin), holding the sieve over the second pan, which should still be off the heat.

6 When the pasta is 2–3 minutes from being al dente, scoop out about 1 cup (8 fl oz/250 ml) of the pasta water and set it aside. Drain the pasta, but not too dry.

7 Return the pan holding the clams to low heat, add the pasta, and toss well with the clams. Add 2 tablespoons or more of the pasta water and continue tossing until the pasta is al dente and a small amount of creamy sauce has formed, about 2 minutes. Mix in the parsley and a swirl of olive oil.

8 Divide the pasta among warmed bowls. The sauce tends to sink to the bottom, so don't serve the first bowl. After filling the second and third bowls, return the first serving back to the pan and mix it with the last, which will have more sauce. Serve at once. Set out extra plates in which diners can dispose of the shells.

Pour a chilled dry white wine that evokes a day at one of Lazio's beaches: Tarquinia DOC or Cerveteri DOC.

FETTUCCINE AL RAGÙ

Fettuccine with Meat Sauce

This easy-to-make meat sauce is comfort food, typical of the Roman trattoria, where, especially on Thursdays, it is also used to sauce gnocchi. The ragù of Rome contains more tomatoes than meat, which distinguishes it from the more famous ragù of Bologna. Nor should the robust fettuccine of Rome be confused with the near-transparent tagliatelle from Emilia-Romagna. While technically a primo piatto, *by today's standards a hearty bowl of* fettuccine al ragù *makes a* piatto unico, *or one-dish meal.*

1 If making the pasta, prepare the dough and roll out as directed in steps 1 and 2 (page 109), but pass it through the next to last roller setting. Then, in step 3, fit the machine with the widest cutter and pass each sheet through the cutter, yielding ribbons ¼–⅜ inch (6 mm–1 cm) wide. Place on lightly floured kitchen towels and dust lightly with flour to prevent sticking.

2 In a large saucepan over low heat, warm the olive oil. Add the celery, carrot, and onion and cook, stirring occasionally, until softened but not browned, about 5 minutes. Add the beef, season with about ½ teaspoon salt and several grinds of pepper, and cook, breaking the meat up with a wooden spoon, until the meat is no longer red, about 10 minutes.

3 Add the wine, raise the heat to high, and bring to a boil. Stir in the tomatoes and their juice, breaking them up with a wooden spoon. Add the bay leaf and return to a boil. Reduce the heat to medium and simmer, uncovered, stirring occasionally, until the sauce is dense and the flavors have blended, about 1½ hours. Discard the bay leaf. Taste and adjust the salt and pepper.

4 Bring a large pot three-fourths full of water (at least 4 qt/4 l) to a rapid boil. Add 1 tablespoon salt and the pasta and stir for the first minute of cooking. Cook the fresh pasta for 2–3 minutes, then drain.

5 Transfer the pasta to a warmed serving bowl, pour the sauce over it, and mix well. Serve in warmed bowls or plates, and pass the cheese at the table.

Serve with a full-bodied red wine such as Merlot.

Pasta dough (page 109) or 1 lb (500 g) fresh fettuccine

2 tablespoons extra-virgin olive oil

1 celery stalk, finely chopped

1 carrot, peeled and finely chopped

1 yellow onion, finely chopped

½ lb (250 g) lean ground (minced) beef

Salt and freshly ground pepper

¼ cup (2 fl oz/60 ml) dry white wine

2 cans (14 oz/440 g each) plum (Roma) tomatoes, with juice

1 bay leaf

Grated Parmigiano-Reggiano cheese for serving

Makes 4–6 servings

Cooking Pasta

Always start with good-quality pasta, whether it is homemade, a package of imported Italian dried, or fresh from a first-rate purveyor. The Italian formula for how much water to use follows a simple metric equation: for each 100 grams pasta, use 1 liter water. This roughly translates to 4 quarts (4 l) water for each pound of pasta. Bring the water to a rolling boil over high heat, add plenty of coarse salt, and then stir in the pasta. Stir almost constantly for the first minute of cooking and occasionally thereafter. Do not add oil to the water; the pasta won't stick if you remember to stir.

The pasta is ready when it is al dente, ("to the tooth," or still chewy). Start checking dried pasta at least 2 minutes before the cooking time on the package. Most fresh pasta cooks very quickly, in 5 minutes or less, and gnocchi are done as soon as they bob to the surface. If you plan to finish the pasta in the pan with the sauce, drain it sooner, since it will continue to cook slightly. Drain pasta gently, using a handheld colander for short varieties. If you are cooking long strands, lift them with a spaghetti fork, and for ravioli, use a slotted spoon.

RAVIOLI DI PESCE CON POMODORINI

Fish Ravioli with Oven-Roasted Cherry Tomato Sauce

The most classic Roman ravioli are filled with ricotta cheese and fresh spinach or with meat (in which case they are called agnolotti). *But ravioli are perfect for experimentation with other fillings, such as game, squab (pigeon), mushrooms, or various cheeses. You can also try other shapes. Instead of small half-moons, as here, make them circular or square. This recipe, inspired by a pasta served at Ristorante Al Presidente, near the Trevi Fountain, relies on the pure taste of the fish. For a deeper flavor in the sauce, roast the tomatoes for up to three hours in a low (250°F/120°C) oven.*

FOR THE SAUCE

8–10 oz (250–315 g) cherry tomatoes

2 tablespoons extra-virgin olive oil

Salt and freshly ground black pepper

2 cloves garlic, chopped

1 cup (8 fl oz/250 ml) homemade or thawed frozen fish stock

FOR THE FILLING

2 tablespoons extra-virgin olive oil

1 leek or 2 green (spring) onions, white part only, chopped

¾ lb (375 g) fish fillets such as rockfish, cod, scrod, red mullet, or monkfish, or lobster meat, cut into 1-inch (2.5-cm) pieces

Salt and ground white pepper

Pasta dough (page 109)

1 large egg yolk, lightly beaten

Salt

Fresh basil leaves for garnish

Makes 4–6 servings

1 Preheat the oven to 350°F (180°C). Put the whole tomatoes in a single layer in a roasting pan. Drizzle with 1 tablespoon of the olive oil and sprinkle with salt and black pepper. Roast the tomatoes until they are soft and shriveled, 45–50 minutes. Remove from the oven and set aside. (This step can be done several days in advance; cover with olive oil and refrigerate.)

2 To make the filling, in a frying pan over medium heat, warm the olive oil. Add the leek and sauté until translucent, 3–5 minutes. Add the fish, reduce the heat to medium, and cook, turning the fish frequently, until opaque throughout, 5–10 minutes. Add a couple of spoonfuls of water if the fish starts to stick, but the pan should be dry when the fish is ready. Season with salt and white pepper. Transfer the fish mixture to a food processor and pulse until it is coarsely chopped, stopping before it becomes a paste. Turn out onto a plate and let cool completely.

3 To finish the sauce, in a sauté pan over medium-high heat, warm the remaining 1 tablespoon olive oil. Add the garlic and cook until golden, 1–2 minutes. Add the fish stock and bring to a boil. Reduce the heat to medium and continue cooking until the stock is reduced slightly. Add the roasted tomatoes and stir over medium heat until the sauce begins to thicken, about 5 minutes. Taste and season with salt and black pepper. Set the pan aside.

4 Meanwhile, prepare the pasta dough as directed in step 1 of page 109. Roll out the dough as described in step 2, but pass it through the narrowest roller setting. Spread the sheets out on a floured work surface. Using a 2½–3-inch (6–7.5-cm) cookie cutter or water glass, cut out at least 28 rounds for about 4 servings. Place 1 teaspoon of the fish filling in the center of each round. Brush the edges of the round with the egg yolk and fold the disk in half, forming a half-moon. Press the edges to seal. Repeat until all the fish is used up. As the ravioli are shaped, set them aside on floured kitchen towels or trays.

5 Return the sauce to low heat. Bring a large pot three-fourths full of water (at least 4 qt/4 l) to a rapid boil over high heat. Add 1 tablespoon salt and the ravioli to the boiling water and stir briefly. When they come to the surface, after 1–2 minutes, use a slotted spoon to transfer them to the sauce. Reserve the pasta water. Gently turn the ravioli in the sauce to coat evenly. If the sauce seems too dry, dilute it with some of the reserved pasta water, adding it 1 tablespoon at a time. Transfer the ravioli to a warmed platter or individual plates. Spoon any additional sauce on top, garnish with basil leaves, and serve at once.

Serve with an important white wine with good structure and some oak, such as the Umbrian Chardonnay Cervaro della Sala.

PASTA AL FORNO

Baked Farfalle with Mushrooms, Prosciutto, and Peas

The Roman category pasta al forno, *literally "baked pasta," includes cannelloni, lasagne, and a host of labor-intensive delicacies, some in a pastry crust, called variously* timballo, pasticcio, *and* timpano. *But sometimes, as here, it is simply unpretentious baked pasta with a sauce.* Pasta al forno *is traditional for Sunday lunch in Rome. This combination of peas, prosciutto, and mushrooms in a* salsa besciamella *(béchamel) is also perfect comfort food for a winter night. Peas are among the only foods that Romans regularly buy frozen and use year-round. When fresh, they never play second fiddle, as they do here.*

1 Preheat the oven to 350°F (180°C). Oil or butter a baking dish with an 2-quart (64-fl oz/2-l) capacity.

2 Cut off the ends of the mushroom stems. Break the stems off where they join the caps and set them aside. Unless the gills are very small and tight, scrape them out with a small knife. Brush the caps clean and lightly peel them if the skins are blemished. Cut each cap into 6 or 8 wedges, depending on the cap's size. Clean and chop the stems.

3 In a large frying pan over medium-low heat, warm 1 tablespoon of the olive oil. Add the shallots and sauté just until they begin to color, about 4 minutes. Stir in the prosciutto and cook for 1 minute longer. Using a slotted spoon, transfer the shallots and prosciutto to a bowl and set aside.

4 Add the remaining 1 tablespoon olive oil to the same pan over medium heat. Add the mushroom caps and stems and sauté until all the liquid they release evaporates and they start to brown, about 8 minutes. Sprinkle with salt. When the mushrooms are golden brown, after about 2 minutes longer, return the prosciutto and shallots to the pan, mix in the peas, and cook for a couple of minutes to blend the flavors. Remove from the heat and set aside in the pan.

5 Bring a large pot three-fourths full of water to a rapid boil over high heat. Add 1 tablespoon salt and the pasta and stir for the first minute of cooking and occasionally thereafter.

6 While the water is heating, make the béchamel sauce. In a saucepan over low heat, melt the butter. Add the flour and cook, stirring constantly, until it starts to brown, about 2 minutes. Very gradually add the milk while stirring constantly, then cook over medium heat, continuing to stir, until the sauce just begins to boil and thicken, about 10 minutes. Stir in 1 teaspoon salt. Remove from the heat, stir into the pea-mushroom mixture, and mix well.

7 When the pasta is 1–2 minutes from being al dente, drain it, but not too dry. Stir the pasta into the sauce in the frying pan. Mix in all but ¼ cup (1 oz/30 g) of the cheese. Spoon the pasta mixture into the prepared baking dish. Dust with the remaining cheese and dot with the butter. (The dish can be made up to this point, covered, and refrigerated for up to 2 days. Bring to room temperature before continuing.)

8 Bake just until the cheese melts, about 15 minutes. Serve piping hot directly from the dish.

Serve with a full-bodied red wine such as a Sangiovese or Merlot from Lazio, Umbria, or Tuscany.

1 lb (500 g) fresh button or cremini mushrooms

2 tablespoons extra-virgin olive oil

2 shallots or 1 small white or yellow onion, thinly sliced

¼ lb (125 g) prosciutto or cooked ham, including some fat, very thinly sliced and then coarsely chopped

Salt and freshly ground pepper

1⅔ cups (8 oz/250 g) frozen petite peas

¾ lb (375 g) farfalle

FOR THE BÉCHAMEL SAUCE

4 tablespoons (2 oz/60 g) unsalted butter

¼ cup (1½ oz/45 g) all-purpose (plain) flour

2 cups (16 fl oz/500 ml) whole milk

Salt

1 cup (4 oz/125 g) grated Parmigiano-Reggiano cheese

1 tablespoon unsalted butter, cut into small pieces

Makes 4–6 servings

GNOCCHI AL GORGONZOLA CON RADICCHIO

Potato Gnocchi with Gorgonzola and Radicchio

In Rome, Thursday is gnocchi day—although no law forbids making the soft potato dumplings any other time. They are usually topped with a simple tomato sauce or meat ragù (page 113), or else served with something fanciful, such as several cheeses or even fish. Gnocchi with Gorgonzola, a blue-veined cheese of Lombardy that dates back to the tenth century, is a delicious pairing seen often throughout Italy. The presence of radicchio provides a touch of color and an element of bitterness. An inexpensive and handy potato ricer, essential to making gnocchi, gives the potatoes the right fluffy consistency.

FOR THE GNOCCHI

2 cups (10 oz/315 g) all-purpose (plain) flour, plus more as needed

2 lb (1 kg) russet or other starchy potatoes

2 tablespoons salt

FOR THE SAUCE

3 cups (6 oz/185 g) coarsely shredded red radicchio leaves

1 tablespoon extra-virgin olive oil

Salt and freshly ground pepper

¼ lb (125 g) *gorgonzola dolce* cheese, cut into small pieces

¼ cup (2 fl oz/60 ml) heavy (double) cream

½ cup (2 oz/60 g) grated Parmigiano-Reggiano cheese

1 tablespoon chopped fresh flat-leaf (Italian) parsley (optional)

Makes 4–6 servings

1 To make the gnocchi, measure out the 2 cups flour into a bowl and place at the edge of a clean work surface. Lay a kitchen towel on a tray or counter near the stove and sprinkle it with more flour. Keep a second clean towel handy.

2 In a saucepan, combine the potatoes with cold water to cover generously. Add the salt and cover; place over medium-high heat and bring to a boil. Cook until quite tender when pierced with the tip of a knife, about 30 minutes. Drain the potatoes and peel them while they are still hot. Immediately put them through a ricer, letting them fall in a mound on the work surface.

3 Using your hands, incorporate the 2 cups flour, little by little, into the potatoes. Keep adding and incorporating the flour until you have a pliable dough that no longer sticks to your hands. (Add more flour as needed.) When the dough is ready, pull or cut off small handfuls. Dusting your palms and the work surface with flour as necessary, roll each handful of dough back and forth against the surface to form a rope about ½ inch (12 mm) in diameter. Cut each rope crosswise into ¾-inch (2-cm) pieces, then press each piece with the tines of a fork, dusting the tines as necessary. As each piece is shaped, place it on the floured towel. Do not allow the gnocchi to touch one another.

4 To make the sauce, in a large, deep frying pan over medium heat, combine the radicchio, olive oil, and 2 tablespoons water. Sprinkle with salt and pepper and cook, stirring, until the leaves have wilted, about 5 minutes. Add more water, 1 tablespoon at a time, if needed to keep the leaves from sticking to the pan. Using a slotted spoon, transfer the radicchio to a bowl and set aside. Reserve the frying pan.

5 Bring a large pot three-fourths full of water (at least 4 qt/4 l) to a rapid boil over high heat. Add 1 tablespoon salt.

6 Return the frying pan to low heat, add the *gorgonzola dolce,* and stir with a wooden spoon until the cheese starts to melt. Add the cream and keep stirring. Return the radicchio to the pan.

7 Drop the gnocchi, a handful at a time, into the boiling water. Keep a careful eye on them, and as soon as they bob to the surface, after about 3 minutes, retrieve them with a slotted spoon and drop them into the pan with the sauce. Stir gently in the sauce to coat. When all of the gnocchi have been added to the sauce, stir in the Parmigiano-Reggiano and sprinkle with the parsley, if using.

8 Transfer the gnocchi to a warmed platter or individual plates and serve at once.

Serve with a fragrant, full-bodied white wine such as a Malvasia or Malvasia blend.

PIZZA CON PEPERONI, POMODORI, E ALICI

Pizza with Roasted Peppers, Tomatoes, and Anchovies

When Romans want to suggest a casual meal with new acquaintances, they say, "Let's have a pizza sometime." Every neighborhood has at least one pizzeria, and the best have wood-burning ovens twice as hot as the average home oven, not to mention talented pizzaioli (pizza makers) who pull and twirl the balls of dough to the size of a plate and a thinness that ensures a crisp crust. Much like ravioli, pizza is the perfect blank slate on which to experiment with different toppings: try wild mushrooms and various cheeses, or a combination of mozzarella and prosciutto or arugula (rocket) in place of the topping here.

1 To make the dough, in a small bowl, stir the yeast into 2 tablespoons lukewarm water. Let stand until creamy, about 3 minutes.

2 On a large work surface, sift together the flours and salt into a mound, then make a well in the center. Pour the yeast mixture, olive oil, and ¼ cup (2 fl oz/60 ml) lukewarm water into the well. Using your fingers or a fork, swirl the liquid in a circular motion, gradually incorporating flour from the sides. Slowly add 1 cup (8 fl oz/250 ml) lukewarm water to the well at the same time, until the ingredients are well combined and a rough dough has formed. Knead vigorously, stretching and pressing the dough against the work surface until it is soft and smooth and comes away cleanly from your hands, about 10 minutes. To check if the dough is sufficiently kneaded, cut off a piece: the cut surface should be pocked with small air holes.

3 Cover the dough with a damp kitchen towel and let rest for 5 minutes. Then divide the dough into 4 balls, cover again, and let rise at room temperature until doubled in volume, about 2 hours.

4 If using fresh tomatoes, preheat the oven to 350°F (180°C). Put the tomatoes in a single layer in a roasting pan. Drizzle with 2 tablespoons of the olive oil and sprinkle with salt and pepper. Roast until soft and shriveled, 45–50 minutes. Set aside.

5 Preheat the broiler (grill). Arrange the bell peppers on a pan and slip under the broiler about 6 inches (15 cm) from the heat source. Broil (grill), turning as needed, until the skin is blistered and charred,

10–15 minutes; watch carefully to avoid burning their flesh. Put the peppers into a paper bag; close the top, and set aside until cool. Cut off the stems and pull off the charred skins. Slit each pepper open lengthwise, remove and discard the seeds and ribs, and cut lengthwise into strips ⅜ inch (1 cm) wide. Set aside.

6 Place a pizza stone or unglazed tiles on the bottom rack of the oven and preheat to 500°F (260°C). Lightly flour the work surface. Place 1 of the dough balls on the work surface, leaving the others under the damp towel. Punch down and flatten into a disk. Turn the disk over, sprinkle with additional flour, and, using a rolling pin or your hands, roll out or stretch the dough into a 12-inch (30-cm) round, turning it over and dusting it regularly with flour as you work.

7 Sprinkle a baker's peel or rimless baking sheet with semolina flour. Gently lay the dough round on top. Cover evenly with one-fourth of the tomatoes or tomato purée and drizzle with 1 tablespoon of the remaining olive oil. Slide the pizza onto the baking stone or tiles and bake until the crust begins to brown, about 5 minutes. Scatter one-fourth of the mozzarella and of the pepper strips over the top and add anchovy fillets. Continue to bake until the cheese is melted and the crust is browned and crisp, about 5 minutes longer. Begin assembling the other 3 pizzas while the first one is baking.

8 Remove from the oven and serve at once. Bake the remaining pizzas in the same way.

Serve with a young local Merlot.

FOR THE DOUGH

1¼ teaspoons active dry yeast

2 cups (10 oz/315 g) all-purpose (plain) flour

2 cups (10 oz/315 g) semolina flour, plus extra as needed

½ teaspoon salt

2 tablespoons extra-virgin olive oil

FOR THE TOPPING

1 lb (500 g) cherry tomatoes, left whole, or ¾ cup (6 fl oz/180 ml) canned plum (Roma) tomato purée

6 tablespoons (3 fl oz/90 ml) extra-virgin olive oil

Salt and freshly ground pepper

2 red bell peppers (capsicums)

1 lb (500 g) fresh mozzarella cheese, shredded or sliced, well drained, and blotted dry

12 olive oil–packed anchovy fillets

Makes 4 servings, or four 12-inch (30-cm) pizzas

SECONDI

Fresh fish from the Tyrrhenian Sea, celery-scented oxtail, and succulent lamb

perfumed with rosemary—the Roman main course is all about flavor.

How better to enhance the taste of a whole fish than to bake it with sliced potatoes? And what could be a tastier way to cook tender lamb than to gently stew it with fresh rosemary? Such thinking is how the meat or fish course of the Roman meal, the *secondo piatto,* acquired its reputation for simple cooking. But it's not all quite so basic. *Saltimbocca alla romana,* thin veal scallops panfried with sage and prosciutto, or stuffed zucchini (courgettes), both perennial favorites, illustrate a slightly greater degree of complexity. You'll find plenty of hearty stews and pot roasts in the local repertory, too.

SALTIMBOCCA ALLA ROMANA

Veal Scallops with Prosciutto and Sage

Saltimbocca means "jump in the mouth," so the dish can safely be presumed to be particularly tasty. Elsewhere in Italy, saltimbocca can mean other recipes, but qualified by alla romana, it refers to thin-sliced veal, prosciutto, and fresh sage, a staple herb of the Roman garden. Some recipes call for folding the layered ingredients in half, while others shape them into neat little involtini (rolls). But the standard procedure, given here, is to secure the sage to the stacked veal and prosciutto with a toothpick.

1 Using a meat pounder, pound the veal slices to flatten them somewhat; they do not need to be paper-thin. Trim the prosciutto slices so they are slightly shorter than the veal slices. Lay a slice of prosciutto on top of each slice of veal, and then top with a sage leaf. Secure the layers together with a toothpick.

2 Spread the flour in a shallow dish. In a large frying pan over medium heat, melt the butter. Dust the veal bundles very lightly and evenly with the flour, shaking off the excess. Working in batches, place the veal, prosciutto side down, in the melted butter and brown gently, about 1 minute. Then turn the veal and brown the other side, about 1 minute. Season with pepper and, if the prosciutto being used is not very salty, season with salt as well. Reduce the heat to medium-low and cook until the veal is cooked through and is a light golden brown, 4–5 minutes.

3 Transfer the veal to a warmed serving platter and tent loosely with aluminum foil to keep warm. When all the veal bundles have been cooked and removed from the pan, raise the heat to medium-high, add the wine, and bring to a boil. Deglaze the pan, allowing most of the liquid to evaporate and scraping up any browned bits from the pan bottom. Pour the hot pan sauce over the veal and serve.

Serve with a rich, flavorful white wine, such as Fiano di Avellino.

12 veal scallops, about 1 lb (500 g) total weight, each about ¼ inch (6 mm) thick

12 very thin prosciutto slices, about ¼ lb (125 g) total weight

12 fresh sage leaves

All-purpose (plain) flour for dusting

2 tablespoons unsalted butter

Salt and freshly ground pepper

½ cup (4 fl oz/125 ml) dry white wine

Makes 4 servings

Herbs of Rome

In Rome, perfuming roasting meat with fresh *rosmarino* (rosemary) is considered so important that butchers typically provide a few sprigs of the herb free of charge. Even without the meat, oven-roasted potatoes are naked without fresh rosemary and garlic. Romans traditionally cook only with fresh herbs, with the exception of bay leaves, which are picked fresh from a pot on the terrace or a tree in the park and left to dry in the kitchen.

Roman cooking is not spicy, except for the occasional use of small dried red chiles. Herbs are usually used one per dish, or mixed only with parsley. This recipe calls for *salvia* (sage), a common ingredient in local cooking. Ask a Roman greengrocer for mint, and he'll inquire, "For artichokes or for tripe?" *La mentuccia,* known elsewhere as *nepitella* (calamint), gives *carciofi alla romana* their minty flavor, while *menta romana,* a kind of spearmint, is essential for *trippa alla romana* and little else.

Basil reigns in summer: It is a principal ingredient in *spaghetti con pomodoro e basilico* and such favorite extraregional imports as *insalata caprese* and traditional *pesto alla genovese.*

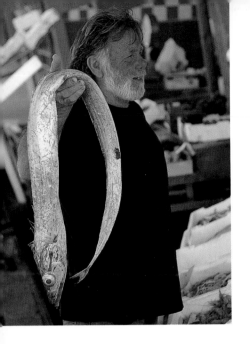

PESCE AL FORNO CON LE PATATE

Baked Whole Fish with Sliced Potatoes

The Romans feel, quite reasonably, that if you have a nice fresh fish, you should honor it with a simple preparation and not make it look, or taste, like anything else. The absence of sauces and condiments takes a little getting used to, but the reward is the subtle flavor and texture of the fish. This recipe is basic, but leaves plenty of room for variation. Instead of onions and parsley, try garlic and rosemary or other herbs, or cherry or grape tomatoes and a bit of marjoram. Instead of a whole fish, use fillets. In Rome, this recipe is often made with orata *(gilthead bream),* spigola *(sea bass), or* dentice *(dentex).*

About 2 tablespoons extra-virgin olive oil

1½ lb (750 g) russet potatoes, peeled and sliced crosswise ⅛ inch (3 mm) thick

Salt and freshly ground pepper, preferably white

1 or 2 whole fish such as sea bass, turbot, cod, or scrod, 2½–3 lb (1.25–1.5 kg) total weight, cleaned with head and tail intact

1 fresh flat-leaf (Italian) parsley sprig

4 lemon slices (optional)

4 white or yellow onions, sliced

Finest extra-virgin olive oil for serving

Makes 4 servings

1 Preheat the oven to 450°F (230°C). Select a shallow baking dish as long as the fish (the fish can be laid diagonally) and brush the dish with some of the olive oil.

2 Spread the sliced potatoes in the bottom of the prepared baking dish, sprinkle them with salt, and drizzle them with a little more of the olive oil. Bake the potatoes, turning them once at the midway point, until they start to brown, about 45 minutes. As they bake, check them occasionally to make sure they are not sticking to the dish.

3 Meanwhile, rinse the fish inside and out and pat dry. Place the parsley and the lemon slices, if using, in the cavity and sprinkle with salt and pepper.

4 When the potatoes have started to brown, remove the baking dish from the oven and reduce the temperature to 250°F (120°C). Using a spatula, move the potatoes to either side of the dish to make room for the fish. Intersperse the onion slices among the potatoes and set the fish in the dish. Drizzle more olive oil over everything. Bake until the fish is opaque throughout when tested with a fork, about 1 hour if using 1 large fish and 30–45 minutes if using 2 smaller fish.

5 Transfer the fish and vegetables to a platter. Fillet the fish and divide evenly among warmed plates. Accompany each serving with some of the potatoes and onions. Offer the head(s) to any connoisseur(s) at your table who wish to pick at the delicate meat. Pass the olive oil bottle at the table.

To highlight the delicate flavor of the fish, serve an unoaked Chardonnay or a Frascati Superiore.

PETTI DI POLLO IN PADELLA

Panfried Chicken Breasts with Herbs

Boneless chicken breasts, which Roman butchers obligingly slice for their customers, are a favorite quick-cooking standby of the city's home cooks—a sprig of rosemary (which the butcher will provide free of charge), a splash of wine, and dinner is ready. This dish, however, requires some advance planning, as the chicken is marinated. The recipe also illustrates an important principle of Italian food: Italian sauces do not rely on elaborate stocks. If you don't have time to make the stock from scratch, you can use canned broth here, and most Italian home cooks would not hesitate to use a bouillon cube.

1 Remove the small fillet (tender) from each chicken breast and save for another use.

2 To make the stock, in a saucepan, combine the chicken wings, carrot, celery, onion, ½ teaspoon salt, a few grinds of pepper, and 2 cups (16 fl oz/ 500 ml) water. Bring to a boil over high heat, skimming off any foam that forms on the surface. Reduce the heat to medium and simmer, uncovered, until reduced by about half, about 10 minutes. Remove from the heat, strain through a fine-mesh sieve, let cool, cover, and refrigerate until needed. Just before using, lift off and discard any fat that has solidified on top. Or, use one 14-fl-oz (430-ml) can prepared chicken broth. Bring the broth to a boil over high heat, reduce the heat to medium-high, and cook, uncovered, until reduced by half, about 6 minutes.

3 While the stock is cooking, in a shallow nonreactive container, combine the olive oil, vinegar, rosemary, bay leaf, ½ teaspoon salt, and a few grinds of pepper and mix well. Add the chicken breasts and turn them to coat well with the marinade. Cover and refrigerate, turning occasionally, for about 2 hours.

4 In a frying pan over medium-high heat, warm 1 tablespoon of the marinade. When it is hot, add the chicken breasts and brown on both sides, about 5 minutes on each side. Reduce the heat to medium and continue cooking until the chicken breasts are opaque throughout when tested with the tip of a knife, about 5 minutes on each side. If the breasts are quite thick, cover the pan and cook for a few minutes longer.

5 Transfer the chicken breasts to a cutting board and let rest for 2–3 minutes. Using a sharp knife, cut against the grain on the diagonal into slices about ½ inch (12 mm) thick. Transfer the slices to a platter.

6 Add the chicken stock to the pan and bring to a boil over high heat. Allow the stock to reduce slightly and scrape up any browned bits on the bottom with a wooden spoon. Season to taste with salt and pepper and spoon the reduced sauce over the chicken slices. Serve at once.

Serve with a Frascati Superiore or one of the IGT white wines from the Castelli Romani.

4 boneless, skinless chicken breast halves

FOR THE STOCK

2 chicken wings

1 carrot

1 small celery stalk

1 small yellow onion

Salt and freshly ground black or green peppercorns

¼ cup (2 fl oz/60 ml) extra-virgin olive oil

1 tablespoon balsamic vinegar

1 tablespoon chopped fresh rosemary

1 bay leaf, crumbled

Salt and freshly ground black or green peppercorns

Makes 4 servings

BACCALÀ IN GUAZZETTO

Salt Cod with Raisins and Pine Nuts in Tomato Sauce

Italy has its fair share of recipes using salt cod, and Rome makes two principal contributions to the collection: this recipe, also called baccalà alla romana, *and batter-fried salt cod fillets, found in pizzerias as an antipasto alongside* fiori di zucca *and in the* fritto misto *of restaurants offering Roman Jewish specialties. This preparation, with raisins and pine nuts, is likely to have migrated north from Sicily. Like fresh fish, salt cod is a standby for meatless Fridays, and even today many food shops presoak the dried fish so their customers can purchase it ready to cook on Friday morning.*

1½ lb (750 g) salt cod fillets

¼ cup (2 fl oz/60 ml) extra-virgin olive oil

About 2 cups (6 oz/185 g) thinly sliced white onion

2 tablespoons pine nuts

2 heaping tablespoons raisins, soaked in warm water for 10 minutes to soften, drained, and squeezed dry

1½ cups (12 fl oz/375 ml) tomato purée

Makes 4 servings

1 Rinse the salt cod well in running cold water, then place it in a large bowl with cold water to cover and refrigerate for 24 hours, changing the water 3 or 4 times. Drain the salt cod and pat dry. Cut each fillet lengthwise down the middle, then cut crosswise at intervals of 2½–3 inches (5–7.5 cm), removing any errant bones or bits of skin. Set aside.

2 In a large frying pan over medium heat, warm the olive oil. Add the onion and sauté until golden brown, 8–10 minutes. Add the cod and cook, turning as needed, until browned on both sides, about 8 minutes total.

3 Add the pine nuts, raisins, and tomato purée to the pan, reduce the heat to low, cover, and cook until the fish is quite tender when pierced with a fork, about 20 minutes. (The dish can be prepared up to this point, cooled, covered, and refrigerated, and then reheated gently the next day.)

4 Transfer the cod and its sauce to a warmed serving dish and serve at once.

Serve with a chilled Chardonnay—either local or from points south (such as Sicily).

STRACCETTI DI MANZO CON RUGHETTA

Sautéed Strips of Beef with Arugula

There is something decadent about this simple preparation of sautéed shredded beef, which became fashionable in the late 1980s, along with the boom in rughetta *(arugula/rocket). The fervor has now cooled, and both* straccetti *and* rughetta *have settled into a permanent spot in the trattoria repertory. The name* straccetti, *"little rags," suggests a dish born in poverty, but it is actually made with the finest lean beef and flavored with balsamic vinegar, the popular condiment that originates in the area around Modena in Emilia-Romagna.*

1 If you have bought unsliced beef, put the beef in the freezer for 20 minutes to make slicing easier, then use a sharp knife to slice the beef as thinly as possible. With your hands or a fork, and working with the grain, tear and shred the beef into bite-sized "rags." Place the beef in a bowl, add 4 tablespoons (2 fl oz/60 ml) of the olive oil, and season with salt and pepper. Toss well and let stand at room temperature for about 15 minutes. Meanwhile, make a bed of the arugula on a platter or individual plates.

2 In a frying pan over medium heat, warm the remaining 2 tablespoons olive oil. Add the mushrooms, raise the heat to medium-high, and sauté until their liquid has evaporated, about 10 minutes. Transfer the mushrooms to a bowl and set aside.

3 Pour off about half of the olive oil from the bowl holding the beef, and place it in the same pan over medium-high heat. When the oil is hot, add the meat and its oil and sprinkle with salt and pepper. Cook, stirring constantly, just until the meat is browned, about 4 minutes. Add the wine and the butter and cook until the liquid in the pan reduces by about half and thickens slightly, 3–4 minutes. (The flour-dusted butter will slightly thicken the pan juices into a sauce.) Return the mushrooms to the pan, reduce the heat to medium, and heat the beef and mushrooms for about 1 minute. Remove from the heat and stir in the vinegar.

4 Spoon the beef and mushrooms and their juices over the arugula. Serve at once.

Serve with one of the Merlot-based Lazio IGT red wines.

1 lb (500 g) boneless lean beef, preferably sliced very thin, with the grain, by the butcher

6 tablespoons (3 fl oz/90 ml) extra-virgin olive oil

Salt and freshly ground pepper

About 2 cups (2 oz/60 g) arugula (rocket), tough stems removed

6–7 oz (185–215 g) fresh button, cremini, porcini (cep), or chanterelle mushrooms, or a combination, brushed clean, trimmed, and cut into small wedges

½ cup (4 fl oz/125 ml) dry white wine

1 tablespoon unsalted butter rolled in all-purpose (plain) flour

2 teaspoons balsamic vinegar

Makes 4–6 servings

Mushrooms

The Italian edible fungus kingdom is divided into two realms, cultivated and wild. Cultivated mushrooms are led by white button mushrooms, which Italians commonly refer to by their French name, *champignon*. They turn up sliced fresh on *pizza ai funghi* and are most typically cooked *trifolati*, sautéed with garlic and parsley. *Cremini*, similar-looking earthy brown mushrooms, are also found in Roman markets. Gray-brown floppy *pleurotus* mushrooms, called *pleos* in the markets of Rome but also known as *geloni*, are available both cultivated and wild and can replace white mushrooms.

The king of wild mushrooms is the stocky brown *porcino*, *Boletus edulis*, which is eaten fresh or dried. The best specimens are sautéed or baked with garlic and oil and served as a *secondo* or on fettuccine. *Porcini* are, however, outranked by the elegant, egg-shaped *ovoli*. In the past, they were so plentiful that people used them in frittatas. Today, pricey *ovoli*, considered too precious to cook, are sliced and served raw with thinly sliced celery, shaved Parmigiano-Reggiano, and fine olive oil.

ARROSTINO DI MAIALE

Roasted Pork with Herbs

It is a common misconception that porchetta *is a suckling pig. In Lazio,* porchetta *is a hog, roasted whole by a specialist* porchettaro. *It is often prepared with large quantities of herbs and sold by the slice with slabs of wonderful* pane casereccio, *the chewy local bread, at street stands like the one opposite the Basilica of San Giovanni in Laterano. The best* porchetta *in Lazio comes from the town of Ariccia, just south of Rome, but just about every fair and festival in the region has a* porchetta *stand. This dainty rolled roast that you can make at home will evoke the aromas of the popular local specialty.*

1¾–2 lb (875 g–1 kg) boneless pork shoulder, rolled and tied

1 clove garlic, cut lengthwise into 6 slivers

2 tablespoons coarsely chopped fresh rosemary

2 tablespoons coarsely chopped fresh sage leaves

Salt and freshly ground pepper

1 tablespoon olive oil

8 boiling potatoes

Makes 4 servings

1 Preheat the oven to 450°F (230°C). Using a small, sharp knife, make 6 small, evenly spaced incisions in the pork. Insert a sliver of garlic, a tiny cluster of rosemary and sage, and a pinch of salt into each incision. Rub the meat all over with the olive oil and grind the pepper on top.

2 Put the pork on a rack in a roasting pan and place in the oven. Fill a saucepan three-fourths full of water, bring to a boil over high heat, add the potatoes, and parboil for 3 minutes. Drain, pat dry, and add the potatoes to the roasting pan, placing them around the pork.

3 When the meat starts to brown, after about 20 minutes, reduce the oven temperature to 350°F (180°C) and continue to roast until the pork is very brown on the outside, cooked through on the inside, and an instant-read thermometer inserted into the thickest part registers 165°F (74°C), about 40 minutes longer. During this time, turn the potatoes as necessary to brown on all sides.

4 Transfer the pork to a cutting board and let rest for 5–10 minutes, away from any drafts. Snip the strings and slice against the grain into slices ¼ inch (6 mm) thick. Divide the pork and potatoes among warmed individual plates and serve at once.

Serve with a flavorful young local red wine such as Cori DOC.

ABBACCHIO ALLA CACCIATORA

Lamb Stewed with Rosemary

The first Romans were shepherds, which means that lamb has been the favorite meat here for close to three thousand years, just as the local cheeses have long been made from sheep's milk. Nearly every trattoria offers abbacchio al forno *(roasted baby lamb) or* scottadito *(tiny grilled chops). Traditionally, no part of the animal goes to waste, and even today butcher shops display lambs' heads and menus offer organ meats such as* coratella *(heart, liver, and lungs) and* animelle *(sweetbreads). This recipe is inspired by the version served at Ristorante Checchino dal 1887, in the Testaccio quarter.*

1 To make the marinade, in a bowl, mix together the vinegar, garlic, rosemary, chile, and salt. Put the lamb pieces in a shallow, nonreactive container and pour the marinade over them. Mix well, cover, and refrigerate for at least 12 hours or for up to 24 hours, stirring occasionally.

2 If using a salt-packed anchovy, rinse it under cool water, trim off the dorsal fin, then open the fish out flat and remove the backbone. Rinse again under cool water, then pat dry.

3 In a heavy frying pan over medium-low heat, warm the olive oil. Add the anchovy fillets and, using a wooden spoon, mash them into the oil. Add the garlic and rosemary, and when the garlic begins to color, after about 2 minutes, raise the heat to high and add the lamb. Sprinkle the lamb with salt and pepper, add the chiles, and brown the lamb on all sides, about 10 minutes total.

4 Pour in the wine and the vinegar, reduce the heat to low, cover, and simmer gently until the lamb is cooked through, about 40 minutes.

5 Using a slotted spoon, transfer the lamb to a warmed serving dish. Raise the heat to high and boil the pan juices for a few minutes to reduce slightly. Using a slotted spoon, remove the rosemary, garlic, and chiles and discard. Pour the pan sauce over the lamb and serve at once.

Serve with a Rosso Lazio IGT made from local grapes, such as Cesanese.

FOR THE MARINADE

½ cup (4 fl oz/125 ml) red wine vinegar

1 clove garlic, cut into several pieces

1 tablespoon coarsely chopped fresh rosemary

1 small dried red chile

½ teaspoon salt

2 lb (1 kg) boneless lamb from leg, cut into 1–1½-inch (2.5–4-cm) pieces

1 salt-packed anchovy or 2 oil–packed anchovy fillets

3 tablespoons extra-virgin olive oil

1 clove garlic, crushed

2 tablespoons coarsely chopped fresh rosemary

Salt and freshly ground pepper

2 small dried red chiles

½ cup (4 fl oz/125 ml) dry white wine

½ cup (4 fl oz/125 ml) red wine vinegar

Makes 4 servings

ZUCCHINE RIPIENE

Stuffed Zucchini

The colorful eggplants (aubergines), peppers (capsicums), and other vegetables of Rome are just begging to be hollowed out and packed with tasty fillings. Zucchini, usually filled with the same beef mixture used for polpette *(meatballs), is served as a main course year-round, but it is best made in summer with* zucchine romanesche *(page 187). This recipe features a vegetarian filling, which includes raisins and pine nuts. An Italian hand tool called a* vuotazucchine *(zucchini emptier) makes quick work of hollowing out the vegetable, but an apple corer works fine, too.*

FOR THE FILLING

6 slices coarse country bread, about 3 oz (90 g) total weight, crusts removed

1 tablespoon extra-virgin olive oil

1 small yellow onion, chopped

1 large egg, lightly beaten

¼ cup (1 oz/30 g) grated *pecorino romano* or Parmigiano-Reggiano cheese

1 tablespoon finely chopped fresh flat-leaf (Italian) parsley

Salt and freshly ground pepper

1 tablespoon pine nuts

1 tablespoon raisins, soaked in warm water for 10 minutes to soften, drained, and squeezed dry

4 unblemished zucchini (courgettes), each at least 1¼ inches (3 cm) in diameter

2 tablespoons extra-virgin olive oil

Salt and freshly ground pepper

1 can (14 oz/440 g) plum (Roma) tomatoes with juice or tomato purée

Makes 4 servings

1 To make the filling, put the bread in the bowl of a food processor and process until fine crumbs form. Leave the bread crumbs in the processor. In a small frying pan over medium heat, warm the olive oil. Add the onion and sauté until translucent, about 8 minutes. Add the onion and its oil to the bread crumbs along with the egg, cheese, parsley, ½ teaspoon salt, and a few grinds of pepper. Process briefly just to mix. Add the pine nuts and raisins and process again for a few seconds. Alternatively, if making by hand, tear the bread slices into soft crumbs and chop the pine nuts and raisins coarsely with a knife, then stir together all the ingredients with a spoon.

2 Trim each zucchini, then cut crosswise into pieces about 3 inches (7.5 cm) long. Using a corer or a small knife, bore a large hole through the middle of each piece. The wall of the resulting cylinder should be about ¼ inch (6 mm) thick. Using the small knife or a spoon, pack the zucchini pieces with the filling.

3 Select a frying pan large enough to accommodate the zucchini pieces in a single layer, add the olive oil, and place over medium-high heat. When it is hot, add the zucchini pieces, laying them on their sides, sprinkle with salt and pepper, and sauté lightly, turning as needed, until just starting to brown on all sides, about 15 minutes. Add the tomatoes and their juice or the tomato purée and about ¼ cup water (2 fl oz/60 ml). Cover and simmer until the zucchini are quite tender when pierced with a knife tip, about 1 hour. Check several times to make sure the zucchini are not sticking; if the pan looks dry, add a little more water.

4 Transfer the zucchini to a serving dish and top with the sauce. Serve at room temperature.

Serve with a young red, such as the local Cesanese.

CODA ALLA VACCINARA
Stewed Oxtail with Tomatoes and Celery

Widely regarded as Rome's most typical meat dish, a robust oxtail stew is the embodiment of quinto quarto *cooking (right). There are many recipes for this classic dish, but everyone agrees that the stew must cook for hours and contain a good deal of celery. Most cooks blanch the oxtails before stewing them. Some use grated chocolate, while others add raisins and pine nuts. This dish tastes even better the next day, when the rich flavors have had time to meld. Save any extra sauce and serve over pasta.*

1 Bring a large pot three-fourths full of water to a boil over high heat and drop in the oxtail pieces. When the water returns to a boil, drain the oxtail pieces and set aside. Finely chop the carrot, onion, and 1 celery stalk. In a large, heavy pot over low heat, warm 2 tablespoons of the olive oil. Add the chopped carrot, onion, and celery and sauté until tender, 8–10 minutes.

2 In a large frying pan over medium-high heat, warm the remaining 3 tablespoons olive oil. Add the oxtail pieces, in batches if necessary, and brown well on all sides, about 15 minutes total. As the pieces are ready, transfer them to the pot holding the vegetables. When all the pieces are browned, sprinkle them with salt. Return the pot to high heat, pour in the wine, and cook until it evaporates, about 10 minutes. Add the tomatoes and their juice, ½ teaspoon salt, and a few grinds of pepper. If the meat is not fully submerged, add water as needed. Reduce the heat to low and simmer, checking the level of liquid occasionally and adding water mixed with tomato paste if needed, until the meat is falling from the bone, about 3 hours.

3 Taste and adjust the seasoning with salt. Cut each remaining celery stalk into 6 pieces and add to the pot. Continue cooking over low heat until the celery is tender, about 30 minutes longer. Remove from the heat and stir in the chocolate. Transfer the oxtail pieces to individual warmed shallow bowls and ladle some of the sauce over them.

Serve with a Barolo, from Piedmont, or a Sangiovese.

2½–3 lb (1.25–1.5 kg) oxtail, in 2-inch (5-cm) pieces, trimmed of excess fat

1 carrot, peeled

1 white or yellow onion

6 celery stalks, or more to taste

5 tablespoons (2½ fl oz/75 ml) extra-virgin olive oil

Salt and freshly ground pepper

1 cup (8 fl oz/250 ml) dry white wine

2 cans (14 oz/440 g each) plum (Roma) tomatoes, coarsely chopped, with juice

1 teaspoon tomato paste, if needed

1 teaspoon grated unsweetened chocolate

Makes 4 servings

Quinto Quarto

Anyone who is put off by animal innards, or offal, at the table can avoid them without difficulty, but they do constitute one of the basic food groups of the traditional Roman kitchen. The collective nickname for what's left over after the carcasses have been quartered is the *quinto quarto,* or "fifth quarter." This kind of cooking is still centered in the Testaccio area, where, in the late nineteenth and early twentieth centuries, workers at the slaughterhouse, *il mattatoio,* on Via di Monte Testaccio, used to receive the hides, tails, and organs of the animals as part of their pay. Local trattorias devised tasty recipes for the innards as well. Some, such as Checchino dal 1887, are still operating today.

Coda alla vaccinara is considered the city's flagship meat dish, but Romans also enjoy *trippa alla romana,* tripe cooked with tomato sauce and mint; and *rigatoni alla pagliata,* the intestines of a milk-fed lamb or calf, still filled with mother's milk, cooked in tomato sauce and tossed with pasta. *Animelle* (sweetbreads) and *rigaglie* (giblets) are popular, as are the heart, liver, and lungs, which together are known as *coratella.*

POLLO ALLA ROMANA CON I PEPERONI
Chicken with Tomatoes and Sweet Peppers

The verb insaporire *sums up an essential concept in Italian cooking. Best translated as "to let the flavor develop," it refers to a process in which the ingredients of a dish take on a bit of one another's flavor. In this recipe, the chicken and peppers are cooked separately and then come together at the end, when each absorbs something from the other, resulting in rich, yet distinctive flavors. This dish was often served on Ferragosto, August 15, the main summer holiday. Sweet, ripe peppers were in season, and meat—even chicken—was considered an indulgence reserved for special occasions.*

1 chicken, about 3 lb (1.5 kg), cut into 8 serving pieces

4 tablespoons (2 fl oz/60 ml) extra-virgin olive oil

2 oz (60 g) prosciutto, including the fat, coarsely chopped

Salt and freshly ground pepper

½ cup (4 fl oz/125 ml) dry white wine

1 can (14 oz/440 g) plum (Roma) tomatoes, coarsely chopped, with juice

2 cloves garlic, crushed

1 tablespoon chopped fresh marjoram

1 large red bell pepper (capsicum), seeded and cut lengthwise into strips ⅜ inch (1 cm) wide

1 large yellow bell pepper (capsicum), seeded and cut lengthwise into strips ⅜ inch (1 cm) wide

Makes 4 servings

1 Rinse the chicken pieces and pat dry. In a large frying pan over low heat, warm 2 tablespoons of the olive oil. Add the prosciutto and sauté until it starts to crisp, about 3 minutes. Add the chicken pieces, raise the heat to medium-high, and brown on all sides, about 15 minutes total. Sprinkle the chicken with the salt and pepper and add the wine to the pan. Cook until the wine evaporates, about 5 minutes. Add the tomatoes, 1 garlic clove, and the marjoram, raise the heat to high, and bring to a boil. Reduce the heat to medium and simmer, uncovered, until the chicken is cooked through, about 20 minutes.

2 Meanwhile, in a second frying pan over medium heat, warm the remaining 2 tablespoons olive oil. Add the remaining garlic clove and cook, stirring occasionally, until golden brown, about 2 minutes. Remove and discard the garlic clove. Add the bell pepper strips and cook, stirring often, until they are tender, about 15 minutes. Remove from the heat.

3 When the chicken is ready, mix the peppers, with all their pan residue, into the chicken, reduce the heat to low, and cook together gently for 5 minutes to blend the flavors.

4 Transfer the chicken and peppers to a warmed serving platter and serve at once.

A young but flavorful red wine is the perfect match, such as a Barbera, from Piedmont, or Cesanese or Olevano Romano from Lazio.

CONTORNI

Spicy sautéed greens, piquant sweet-and-sour onions, tender artichokes—

it's a pity to keep vegetables this good on the sidelines.

In a traditional Italian restaurant, the main dish arrives alone on the plate, so you need to order any vegetable side dish, or *contorno,* separately. Preparations for these dishes tend to be quick and simple, though some Roman classics, such as caramelized onions or braised artichokes, take a bit more care. Portions are often hearty, and for vegetarians or anyone eating light, the *contorno* can stand in for the meat course. It might be a salad or sautéed greens in winter, or romano beans slowly braised with ripe tomatoes in summer.

INSALATA ROSSA

"Red Salad" of Tomatoes, Carrots, and Red Onions

Italian menus often follow the flag—the sauce is red, the pasta is white, and the salad is green. But when the pasta is dressed in green, the salad should be red. In the Roman summer, when the luxurious growth of basil on the city's balconies and terraces makes emerald pesto alla genovese *a favorite pasta sauce, this bright red salad follows it nicely. The tomatoes are full of flavor, and sweet red Tropea onions from Calabria are available in the markets. Accompany the salad with bread for soaking up the juices.*

1 If using large tomatoes, core them, then cut them in half crosswise and into wedges. If using medium-sized tomatoes, core and cut into wedges through the stem end. If using cherry or grape tomatoes, core and cut into halves or quarters (depending on the size) through the stem end. Set the tomatoes aside.

2 Using a mandoline, the slicing blade of a food processor, or a cheese slicer, cut the carrots into very thin rounds and place in a salad bowl.

3 Add the onion to the carrots, then season to taste with salt and pepper. Mix in the vinegar to taste, if using, and then the olive oil. (In Italy, tomatoes tend to be quite acidic, and vinegar is typically not used. If your tomatoes have no bite at all, you will probably want to use a small amount, ½–1 teaspoon.) Add the tomato pieces and the torn basil leaves and stir to mix.

4 Divide the salad among individual plates and serve. (The salad can be assembled an hour or so before serving, but in that case, add the salt and the vinegar, if using, at the last moment and toss just before serving.)

2 large or 3 medium tomatoes, preferably an heirloom variety, or about 16 cherry or grape tomatoes

4 young, tender carrots

1 small sweet red onion or 2 or 3 green (spring) onions, white parts only, thinly sliced

Salt and freshly ground pepper

Balsamic or red wine vinegar (optional)

1 tablespoon extra-virgin olive oil

A few fresh basil leaves, torn into pieces

Makes 4 servings

Tomatoes

While fresh tomatoes are available year-round, most Romans buy them only at the height of summer, when the locally grown *pomodori* are in the city's markets, sometimes mixed with "imports" from Campania, Apulia, and Sicily. During the winter, Italians prefer to use tomatoes and tomato purée packed in bottles, cans, or asceptic boxes, rather than rely on the hothouse harvest for their sauces.

In warm weather, large red tomatoes, labeled *da riso* in the markets, are filled with rice, baked, and serve as a *primo piatto*. Local custom dictates that salad tomatoes be firm and a bit green. Bright red spherical tomatoes still on the stem are favored for sauces, as is the sweet, oval San Marzano, which is cultivated in the warm countryside south of Rome. The small, pumpkin-shaped Casalino, eaten very ripe, is superb cut in halves or chunks and squashed onto bruschetta or tossed in pasta—always with fresh basil. Many varieties of *ciliegino* (cherry tomato), notably those from Pachino, in Sicily, and slightly larger tomatoes, sometimes sold still on the branch, turn up on pizza, pasta, alongside baked fish, and in salads.

VERDURA STRASCINATA

Greens with Garlic and Chile

Green leafy vegetables are an integral part of the Italian diet, especially in the winter, when spinach, broccoli rabe, and wild greens are at their best. Anything tender enough to be eaten raw can be tossed into a salad, and the rest is customarily boiled and treated in one of two ways: all'agro, *dressed at the table with olive oil and a squeeze of lemon juice, or* strascinata *(literally, "dragged"), also referred to as* ripassata in padella, *sautéed with garlic and chile. Only spinach is handled differently: briefly steamed and served* all'agro, *with butter, or sautéed with raisins and pine nuts.*

1 lb (500 g) broccoli rabe or other leafy green vegetable

Salt

2 tablespoons extra-virgin olive oil

2 cloves garlic, chopped

1 small dried red chile, cut into pieces, or ½ teaspoon red pepper flakes

Makes 4–6 servings

1 Pick over the greens carefully, discarding any yellow leaves. Trim away any tough stems. Rinse well.

2 Bring a large pot three-fourths full of water to a rapid boil. Add 1 tablespoon salt and the greens and boil until the greens are tender, 6–8 minutes. Using a slotted spoon or skimmer, lift the greens out of the water and set them gently in a colander. Do not press or squeeze them: they should stay fairly wet. (The cooking water, filtered to remove any residual grit, can be reserved for another use, such as soup.)

3 In a large frying pan over medium-high heat, warm the olive oil. When it is hot, add the garlic and chile and cook, stirring occasionally, for about 2 minutes. Add the boiled greens to the oil in the pan, reduce the heat to medium, and sauté until all the water from the greens has evaporated, 7–10 minutes.

4 Transfer the greens to a warmed serving dish and serve at once.

€ 250

CIPOLLINE IN AGRODOLCE

Sweet-and-Sour Onions

Romans have had a taste for sweet and sour since ancient times, when honey, grape must, or sweet wine provided the sweet, and vinegar or garum (right) the sour. In traditional Roman cooking, wild boar or beef tongue may be cooked in agrodolce, as are occasionally red mullet and salt cod. These onions, cooked until golden brown and tender, are ubiquitous in Rome during the colder months. This recipe yields piquant onions that nicely complement the simply prepared meats that are so much a part of the Roman menu.

1 To peel the onions, cut off the root end and remove the papery skin and, if it is blemished, the outer layer. (Holding them under cold running water as you work helps prevent tears.) Alternatively, bring a pot three-fourths full of water to a rapid boil over high heat. Add the onions, boil for 1 minute, drain, and immerse in cold water to cool. Cut off the root end from each onion and then squeeze the onion; it should slide from its skin. Cut away any tenacious skin at the top. Rinse to remove any residual skin or dirt.

2 Place the onions in a heavy saucepan or deep frying pan large enough to accommodate them in a single layer. Pour the oil over them, add the sugar, ¼ teaspoon salt, vinegar, wine, and ½ cup (4 fl oz/ 125 ml) water, and stir just to mix.

3 Place the pan over medium heat and bring to a boil. Reduce the heat to medium-low and simmer, uncovered, until much of the liquid has evaporated and a thick sauce remains in the pan, about 1 hour. The onions should be quite tender and golden brown.

4 Transfer to a serving bowl and serve warm or at room temperature. They will keep nicely, tightly covered, in the refrigerator for a few days.

1 lb (500 g) small, flat onions such as Cipolline or Borettana, or small boiling onions

2 tablespoons extra-virgin olive oil

¼ cup (2 oz/60 g) sugar

Salt

½ cup (4 fl oz/125 ml) white wine vinegar

½ cup (4 fl oz/125 ml) dry white wine

Makes 4 small servings

The Ancient Roman Kitchen

The ancient Roman diet was based on vegetables, fresh cheeses, whole grains, fruits, chicken and fish, olives and olive oil, plenty of herbs and spices, and wine—not a bad diet, all around. And yet, the Roman kitchen has endured centuries of bad press due to exaggerated descriptions of some extravagant dinner parties, and to Pliny the Elder's careless remark, in the first century AD, that *garum,* a popular fish sauce of the time, was made from rotten fish.

In fact, the recipe called for curing small fish under salt and herbs—not unlike modern salt-packed anchovies—for three weeks. The liquid that resulted was the *garum,* which proved so important to ancient Rome that fortunes were made in its manufacture, notably at Pompeii.

Aside from some common ingredients, no continuous line can be drawn between the cooking of antiquity and the Roman food ways of today. But there are some coincidental similarities: sheets of dried dough were layered with cheese and other ingredients in a protolasagna, and grape must and vinegar were used as a sweet-and-sour flavoring.

INSALATA VERDE

Salad of Roman Field Greens

This green salad, a variation of misticanza *(page 44), which takes advantage of the edible wild greens of the countryside around Rome, is meant to be a refreshing palate cleanser before dessert. Use the wildest salad greens you can find, though their cultivated cousins will do in a pinch.* Raperonzoli *(rampions), small white roots with leafy tops, which appear in Roman market stalls in the fall and winter, are popular additions. The dressing is mixed directly on the salad, never on the side, and should consist of the best extra-virgin olive oil and red wine vinegar you can find.*

5 cups (6½ oz/200 g) tender wild or cultivated salad greens such as arugula (rocket), mâche, radicchio, escarole (Batavian endive), and watercress, in any combination

3 green (spring) onions, white parts only, thinly sliced

Salt and freshly ground pepper

2 teaspoons red wine vinegar

2 tablespoons extra-virgin olive oil

Makes 4 servings

1 Pick over the greens carefully, discarding any discolored leaves. Trim away any tough stems.

2 Put the green onions in the bottom of a large salad bowl. Sprinkle with salt and pepper, and add the vinegar and then the oil. Mix vigorously with a fork.

3 Lay the greens on top of the green onions and sprinkle with a little more salt. The salad can sit like this for an hour or so before serving.

4 Just before serving, toss the salad well, making sure to coat the leaves evenly with the oil. Add a little more olive oil if the leaves are not all lightly glistening, being careful not to add too much.

CARCIOFI ALLA ROMANA

Braised Whole Artichokes

This dish of braised artichokes—the standard-bearer of traditional Roman vegetables—is remarkable for three things: the mystique of the carciofo romanesco *(large Roman globe artichoke), the special way the artichoke is cut, and the distinctive mintlike* mentuccia *(Roman dialect for* nepitella, *or calamint in English). Unfortunately, not everyone has access to real Roman artichokes (or* mentuccia*). Just buy the most tender artichokes available and aggressively remove anything that isn't edible. A* carciofo alla romana *should have an almost buttery texture. The more olive oil you use, the better the dish will be.*

1 Fill a bowl with water and squeeze the juice of the lemon into it. Working with 1 artichoke at a time, trim off the base of the stem, leaving at least 2 inches (5 cm) attached, then peel away the stem's dark, stringy outer layer. Remove all the tough outer leaves until you reach the pale, tender inner leaves. Hold the artichoke in one hand and a small, sharp knife in the other. Rest the artichoke against the knife blade without pressing and turn the artichoke against the blade. Then cut about ½ inch (12 mm) off the top. (The process may seem wasteful, but what remains is the most tender, edible part.) As you finish trimming each artichoke, drop it into the lemon water.

2 On a cutting board, using a mezzaluna (a two-handled curved chopping knife), finely chop together the herb(s) and the garlic clove, if using. (Alternatively, use a chef's knife or a small food processor.) Transfer to a small bowl, add 2 tablespoons of the olive oil and ¼ teaspoon salt, and mix well.

3 If the artichokes are tender, spread the leaves apart with your fingers to expose the center and pull out a bit of the choke to create a small cavity. If they are not tender, the easiest way to expose the center is to push an apple corer deep into the middle of the artichoke to cut out a plug of center leaves and some of the choke. Alternatively, you can pry out the leaves and choke with a spoon.

4 Using a small spoon, put about 2 spoonfuls of the herb mixture into each artichoke and reserve the rest. Place the artichokes, stem up, in a heavy pot

large enough to hold them snugly in a single layer and tall enough to accommodate the stems. Sprinkle the remaining herb mixture over the artichokes, then drizzle them with the remaining 2 tablespoons olive oil, or a little more. Place over medium heat and brown lightly on the bottom, about 5 minutes. Pour in the wine to a depth of not more than ½ inch (12 mm).

5 Cover the pot and place over medium heat, preferably with a flame diffuser. When the liquid boils, turn the heat to low. Put a folded brown-paper bag or a folded kitchen towel over the top of the pot, making sure to keep its edges away from the burner, and top with the pot lid. This will draw off moisture so the artichokes will not taste boiled. Finally, place a weight, such as a stone or a meat tenderizer, on the lid to keep it as tight-fitting as possible. Cook the artichokes until they are quite tender. This will take up to 40 minutes, depending on how young and tender they are. Check the level of the wine 2 or 3 times while they cook, and add a little more if the pot is dry.

6 When the artichokes are tender, uncover and let any remaining liquid evaporate. Let the artichokes continue cooking for a couple of minutes in the oil that remains in the pan. Transfer the artichokes to a serving plate and pour any oil remaining in the pot over the top. Serve warm or at room temperature.

½ **lemon**

4 **young, tender artichokes**

3 **tablespoons fresh** *nepitella* **(see note), peppermint, pennyroyal, or flat-leaf (Italian) parsley leaves, or a combination**

1 **clove garlic (optional)**

4 **tablespoons (2 fl oz/60 ml) extra-virgin olive oil, or as needed**

Salt

About ½ **cup (4 fl oz/125 ml) dry white wine**

Makes 4 servings

PUNTARELLE CON LA SALSA

Puntarelle with Anchovy Dressing

Only a few years ago, the word puntarelle *was practically unknown outside the Eternal City. Winter visitors to Rome returned home with tales of a fascinating salad of fresh bitter greens with anchovy dressing. Summer visitors never found out what they were talking about. Today, pale green* puntarelle, *a variety of Catalonian chicory, with long, spiky, dark leaves, are still available only in the colder months, but they are now well known throughout Italy. In the off-season, some Romans pair other salad greens with the* salsa. *Crisp frisée is probably the best substitute when* puntarelle *are not available.*

1 head *puntarelle*, chicory (curly endive), or frisée

1 clove garlic

2 salt-packed anchovies or 3 olive oil-packed anchovy fillets

1 teaspoon red wine vinegar

3 tablespoons extra-virgin olive oil

Makes 4 servings

1 If using *puntarelle,* remove the leafy external stalks, then separate the inner stalks that have buds on top. Discard the tough lower part of each stalk. Cut off the buds and slit the lower part of the bud all around, to create a daisy effect. Peel away the outer fibers of the remaining stalk, then cut the stalk lengthwise into 4 or 5 strips, each about ⅛ inch (3 mm) wide. Rinse well. Immerse the pieces in ice water until they start to curl, about 30 minutes, then drain and dry well. If you are using another variety of chicory, tear the leaves into bite-sized pieces, rinse, and dry well. Place the greens in a salad bowl.

2 Cut the garlic clove in half lengthwise, remove any green shoot, and then coarsely chop and place in a mortar. Using a pestle, grind the garlic. If using anchovies packed in oil, add to the mortar. If using salt-packed anchovies, rinse each fish under cool run-ning water, trim off the dorsal fin, and then open the fish out flat and remove the backbone. Rinse the fillets under cool water, set 1 aside for another use, and add the remaining 3 fillets to the mortar. Pound the anchovy fillets to a rough paste. Mix in the vinegar and then the olive oil.

3 Just before serving, pour the contents of the mortar over the greens and toss to coat the leaves evenly. Serve at once.

FAGIOLI A CORALLO IN UMIDO

Romano Beans with Tomatoes

In Italian, fagioli *usually refers to beans removed from a pod, such as white cannellini beans, while* fagiolini *have an edible pod, such as green beans. Yet it seems to bother no one that the long, flat, completely edible romano beans used in this recipe go by both names,* fagioli a corallo *and* fagiolini a corallo, *with a slight preference for the former in the markets of Rome. Nor does anyone explain the* corallo, *which means "coral," though it may reflect the fact that the beans turn reddish when left to dry on the plant.*

1 In a saucepan large enough to hold the beans, warm the olive oil over medium-low heat. Add the green onions and cook, stirring, until translucent, about 8 minutes. Add the tomatoes and the chile, if using, raise the heat to medium, and simmer, stirring occasionally, until the tomatoes reduce slightly, about 10 minutes.

2 Stir in the beans and sprinkle with salt and a few grinds of pepper. Reduce the heat to low, cover, and cook until the beans are very tender, about 30 minutes. Check frequently and add 2 tablespoons hot water if the sauce looks dry. (The dish can be prepared up to this point, cooled, covered, and refrigerated, and then reheated gently the next day. It will taste even better the second day.)

3 Transfer the beans to a warmed serving dish and sprinkle with the parsley, if using. Serve at once.

1–2 tablespoons extra-virgin olive oil

3 green (spring) onions, white parts only, thinly sliced

½ lb (250 g) very ripe fresh tomatoes, peeled, seeded, and diced, or 1 can (14 oz/440 g) plum (Roma) tomatoes, coarsely chopped, with juice

1 small dried red chile (optional)

1 lb (500 g) romano beans or green beans, ends trimmed

Salt and freshly ground pepper

1 tablespoon finely chopped fresh flat-leaf (Italian) parsley (optional)

Makes 6 servings

Legumes

Legumes have an important place on the Roman menu. *Pasta e ceci (page 93),* chickpeas (garbanzos) combined with short pasta and a little tomato, is perhaps the most beloved dish in town. A pot of lentils, symbolizing coins, is traditionally served on New Year's Eve, while lentils mixed with an equal amount of rice or pasta is a hearty soup the rest of the year. Dried or fresh *fagioli borlotti,* red-freckled beans similar to cranberry beans, star in *pasta e fagioli.* Their pink-marbled pods are a feature of markets in summer, when the fresh beans are boiled and dressed with oil and vinegar and mixed with slices of red onion. White cannellini beans are cooked with pork rinds and tomatoes for hearty *fagioli con le cotiche.* Hard-to-find *cicerchia* (chickling vetch), which looks like a squared-off, flattened chickpea, is usually used for soup.

No one has more fun with fava (broad) beans than the Romans. Early in the season, when the beans are still small and tender, they are shelled at the table and popped into the mouth raw between bites of *pecorino romano* cheese. Later, they are simmered with *guanciale.*

DOLCI

In Rome, almost any event or time of day is right for serving something sweet—

like hazelnut *tozzetti*, crumbly fruit *crostata,* or rich, custardy *zuppa inglese.*

Ricotta, hazelnuts (filberts), pine nuts, wild strawberries, sour cherries—the ingredients in Rome's sweets often come from the nearby countryside. A bowl of fresh fruit is the usual close to a meal, though a slice of pineapple has supplanted it in recent years. Most creative restaurants offer a menu of tempting desserts, many of them chocolate, but it is more common to find traditional sweets such as *torta di ricotta* in a *pasticceria* or private home. Trattorias and classic restaurants typically rely on a few old favorites, such as a tiramisù or crème caramel.

FRAGOLE CON IL "MOUSSE" DI RICOTTA

Strawberries with Ricotta Mousse

In Rome, nothing evokes summer better than capping off a dinner with a dish of fresh fragole (strawberries) or fragoline di bosco (wild strawberries). The best are from the town of Nemi, which sits on a picturesque rise above a lake of the same name, southeast of Rome. A scoop of crema (custard) gelato or a squeeze of lemon juice and spoonful of sugar are the usual accompaniments for the berries, but their partner in this recipe is a sweet and decadent mix of ricotta, mascarpone cheese, and whipped cream.

1 If the ricotta is very fresh and still throwing off clear liquid, spoon it into a colander or a piece of cheesecloth (muslin) and suspend over a bowl. Cover it and leave it to drain in the refrigerator until it is quite dry, which can take up to 24 hours. (If using commercial ricotta, skip this step.) For a smoother texture, remove the ricotta from the refrigerator and force through a coarse-mesh sieve placed over a bowl. For a more rustic texture, use the drained ricotta as is.

2 In a large bowl, combine the ricotta, mascarpone, granulated sugar, and rum. Using a rubber spatula, mix until well blended.

3 In another bowl, using a balloon whisk or handheld mixer on medium-high speed, beat the cream until soft peaks form. Using the spatula, gently fold the whipped cream into the ricotta mixture until blended.

4 Have ready six 1-cup (8–fl oz/250-ml) glass bowls or goblets. Spoon the ricotta mixture into the bowls, dividing it evenly. Cover and refrigerate for at least 2 hours or up to 24 hours to let the flavors meld.

5 About 1 hour before serving, place the strawberries in a bowl, stir in the confectioners' sugar, cover, and refrigerate until serving.

6 To serve, stir the vinegar into the strawberries. Top each portion with the berries and their juices. Garnish with mint and serve at once.

Bring out the fruit flavor with a chilled Brachetto d'Acqui.

FOR THE MOUSSE

1 lb (500 g) whole milk ricotta cheese, preferably fresh

8 oz (250 g) mascarpone cheese

⅔ cup (5 oz/155 g) granulated sugar

¼ cup (2 fl oz/60 ml) rum or brandy

1 cup (8 fl oz/250 ml) heavy (double) cream

1 lb (500 g) strawberries, hulled and quartered lengthwise

2 tablespoons confectioners' (icing) sugar

1 teaspoon white wine or champagne vinegar

Fresh mint leaves for garnish

Makes 6–8 servings

Fruit

Fruit is a hallmark of Roman food culture, as evidenced in the fruit bowl for dessert, the glass of juice at a bar, or even the *frullato* (fruit-flavored milk shake) or fruit gelato at the *gelateria*.

When the bright orange *nespole* (medlars) and deep-red *ciliegie* (cherries) appear, spring is turning into summer. *Fichi* (figs), destined to be peeled and eaten with prosciutto, arrive with the first heat of June and make an encore in September. Big *cantalupo* or small *francesino* melons keep the prosciutto company in between. *Albicocche, pesche,* and *susine* (apricots, peaches, and plums) are plentiful at summer's midpoint, but throughout the season, Romans feast on wild and cultivated strawberries and sweet *cocomero* (watermelon).

When the brown-flecked Muscat grapes appear, summer is turning into fall. Juicy *fichi d'India* (prickly pears) come up from the south, but *kaki* (persimmons) can grow in Roman backyards. Winter means *mele* (apples), from the northeast; *pere* (pears), often cooked in wine; and the prized *tarocchi,* sweet blood oranges from Calabria and Sicily.

TORTA DI RICOTTA

Ricotta Tart

Ricotta is made in part from whey, a by-product of cheese making. Because of this, it is not considered a true cheese, but instead a latticino, *or dairy product. While cow's milk ricotta is the most common, and ricotta made from water buffalo's milk and goat's milk is found as well, rich, creamy* ricotta romana, *made from sheep's milk (page 181), is particularly prized by Roman cooks. It is a popular filling for such sweets as* sfogliatelle *(filled flaky pastry) and* cannoli, *and for tarts, such as this recipe adapted from a dessert made by Enrico Licata, the talented pastry chef at Ristorante La Piazzetta, just off Via Cavour.*

FOR THE FILLING

3 cups (1½ lb/750 g) whole-milk ricotta cheese, preferably fresh

¾ cup (6 oz/185 g) granulated sugar

1 teaspoon Strega or Sambuca liqueur or light rum

1½ oz (45 g) bittersweet chocolate, shaved with a knife

FOR THE PASTRY DOUGH

¾ cup (6 oz/185 g) unsalted butter, at room temperature, cut into ¾-inch (2-cm) pieces

1¾ cups (7 oz/220 g) confectioners' (icing) sugar, sifted

2 tablespoons honey

⅛ teaspoon vanilla extract (essence)

Grated zest of 1 lemon

Pinch of salt

3 large egg yolks, plus 1 more yolk for brushing, lightly beaten

3 cups (12 oz/375 g) cake (soft-wheat) flour, sifted

1 teaspoon baking powder

Makes one 11-inch (28-cm) tart, or 8 servings

1 If the ricotta is very fresh and still throwing off clear liquid, follow the instructions in step 1 on page 169. (If using regular commercial ricotta, skip this step.)

2 To make the pastry dough, in a bowl, combine the butter, confectioners' sugar, honey, vanilla, lemon zest, and salt. Using your fingers, quickly work the ingredients together just until mixed. Using a wooden spoon, quickly work in the 3 egg yolks. In a small bowl, whisk together the flour and baking powder. Gradually stir the flour mixture into the butter mixture. As soon as the ingredients come together, pat into a rough mass. Cover the bowl with plastic wrap and refrigerate the dough for at least 2 hours or for up to 24 hours.

3 Have ready an 11-inch (28-cm) pie pan or tart pan with a removable bottom. Work the dough briefly to form a smooth mass, then divide into 2 pieces, one slightly larger than the other. Form each piece into a disk, and refrigerate the smaller disk. Place the larger disk on a lightly floured work surface, and roll out into a round about 12½ inches (31.5 cm) in diameter and ¼ inch (6 mm) thick. If the dough becomes too soft, return it to the refrigerator to chill until firm. Drape the round over the rolling pin and carefully ease it into the pan, gently pressing it into the bottom and up the sides. Using the tip of a sharp knife, cut around the inside edge of the pan bottom, leaving just a circle of pastry in the bottom and freeing the dough on the sides. Gather the removed strip of dough, pat into a ball, and then roll back and forth against the floured work surface to create a rope

½–¾ inch (12 mm–2 cm) in diameter and 35 inches (88 cm) long (the circumference of the pan). Lay this rope around the inside edge of the pan, resting it on the pastry bottom. (The rope is used to form a shallow, decorative reinforced edge to the tart.) Using the tines of a fork, press against the rope to make a ridged pattern, and prick the bottom crust in several places. Cover and refrigerate.

4 Preheat the oven to 375°F (190°C). To make the filling, put the ricotta in a bowl and beat vigorously with a wooden spoon to soften. Add the granulated sugar, beat well to combine, and then let the mixture rest for 5 minutes. Stir in the liqueur and chocolate. Spoon the filling into the pastry-lined pan and spread it evenly. Remove the smaller disk from the refrigerator and divide the dough into 10 balls. Using the same technique you used for the rolling the rope for the edge of the tart, roll each ball into a rope ¼–½ inch (6–12 mm) wide and 11 inches (28 cm) long. Lay 5 ropes across the filling. Lay the remaining 5 ropes across the first ropes to create a lattice pattern. Cut off any excess dough and discard it. Brush the ropes with the remaining beaten egg yolk.

5 Bake the tart until the crust is a deep golden brown and the filling is set, 40–45 minutes. Transfer to a wire rack and let cool. Cut into wedges and serve at room temperature.

Serve with a dessert wine such as Moscato Passito di Pantelleria, from an island off Sicily.

TOZZETTI

Hazelnut Biscotti

Tozzetti take their name from tozzo, "stale bread," an allusion to their crunchy, crumbly character. They belong to the Lazio tradition of homemade dry sweets, which also includes various biscotti made with milk and eaten for breakfast, or with wine, such as ciambelline al vino (page 61). Tozzetti are distinguished from Tuscany's almond-laced cantucci by the use of hazelnuts, an important product of northern Lazio. These biscotti are a staple of the city's pasticcerie, so only dedicated bakers make them at home today. Serve them with a sweet wine in late afternoon or after dinner or with morning coffee.

1 Preheat the oven to 300°F (150°C). Spread the hazelnuts in a single layer on a baking sheet and toast, shaking the pan every 10 minutes, until the nuts darken and give off a strong aroma, 25–30 minutes. Pour them out onto a plate to cool. (There is no need to remove the skins.) Put one-third of the cooled nuts into a food processor and pulse to chop very finely (do not process to a powder). Set aside.

2 In a large bowl, whisk together the eggs and sugar until well blended. Stir in the melted butter. Add the finely chopped nuts and mix well. Add the flour and salt and mix well. Finally, add the whole hazelnuts and stir to distribute them evenly. At this point, the dough will be very stiff.

3 Preheat the oven to 350°F (180°C). Line a large rimmed baking sheet or two smaller baking sheets with parchment (baking) paper.

4 Transfer the dough to a floured work surface. Divide the dough into 4 pieces. Form each portion into a rectangle about ¾ inch (2 cm) thick, 2 inches (5 cm) wide, and about 6 inches (15 cm) long, or as long as your longest spatula. Using the spatula, transfer the rectangles to the prepared baking sheet, spacing them about 2 inches (5 cm) apart.

5 Bake the rectangles, watching to make sure the bottoms do not get too brown, until the top of each is firm to the touch, about 30 minutes. Remove from the oven and, using the spatula, transfer the rectangles to a cutting board. Let cool slightly, then, using a large knife, cut each rectangle on the diagonal into slices ⅝ inch (1.5 cm) thick. Place the slices, with a cut side down, on the baking sheet (if all the slices won't fit, bake them in 2 batches). Bake until the cookies color slightly and are quite firm, 20–25 minutes longer.

6 Transfer the cookies to a wire rack and let cool completely. Store in an airtight container at room temperature for up to several weeks.

Dip the biscotti in a sweet Aleatico di Gradoli, their historic partner. Vin Santo, a more widely available sweet wine from Tuscany, is a fine substitute.

2 cups (10 oz/315 g) hazelnuts (filberts)

3 large eggs

1½ cups (12 oz/375 g) sugar

6 tablespoons (3 oz/90 g) unsalted butter, melted and cooled

3 cups (15 oz/470 g) all-purpose (plain) flour

⅛ teaspoon salt

Makes about 4 dozen cookies

ZUPPA INGLESE

Sponge Cake with Custard and Liqueur

Most connoissuers of Italian food know that the name of this popular dessert means "English soup," which it was supposedly given for its resemblance to British trifle. However, few know that one of the ingredients, alchermes, a bright red, herb-and-spice-flavored liqueur invented by Florentine monks, derives its name from the Arabic qirmiz, which is also the source of the English word crimson. The composition of zuppa inglese may vary, the only constants being cake, custard, and alcohol, preferably some of it red. To save time and labor, use a store-bought sponge cake.

FOR THE SPONGE CAKE

4 large eggs, separated

⅓ cup (3 oz/90 g) granulated sugar

Pinch of salt

⅓ cup (1½ oz/45 g) cake (soft-wheat) flour

1 teaspoon baking powder

FOR THE CUSTARD

2 cups (16 fl oz/500 ml) whole milk

1 large lemon zest strip

1 large whole egg plus 3 large egg yolks

⅓ cup (3 oz/90 g) granulated sugar

¼ cup (1½ oz/45 g) all-purpose (plain) flour

1 teaspoon Sambuca

¼ cup (2 fl oz/60 ml) rum, or more to taste

¼ cup (2 fl oz/60 ml) *alchermes* (see note) or framboise

½ cup (4 fl oz/125 ml) heavy (double) cream

2 teaspoons confectioners' (icing) sugar

About 2 teaspoons grated bittersweet chocolate

Makes 4 servings

1 To make the sponge cake, preheat the oven to 375°F (190°C). Butter an 8-inch (20-cm) cake pan, dust with flour, and tap out the excess.

2 In a bowl, using a handheld mixer on medium speed, beat together the egg yolks and granulated sugar until thick and pale yellow, about 5 minutes. When the beaters are lifted, the mixture should fall from them in a ribbon that slowly dissolves on the surface. In a large bowl, using the mixer with clean beaters, beat the egg whites until frothy. Add the salt and beat until firm peaks form.

3 In a small bowl, whisk together the flour and baking powder. Using a rubber spatula, gradually fold the flour mixture into the yolk mixture. Stir about one-third of the whites into the yolk mixture, and then gently fold in the remaining whites just until no white streaks remain. Pour the batter into the prepared pan.

4 Bake the cake until a toothpick inserted into the center comes out clean, about 30 minutes. Transfer to a wire rack, let cool for about 10 minutes, and then turn the cake out onto the rack.

5 While the cake is baking, make the custard. In a saucepan over medium heat, combine the milk and lemon zest strip and heat until small bubbles appear along the edges of the pan. Remove from the heat, let cool slightly, and then remove and discard the lemon zest. Meanwhile, in a bowl, whisk together the whole egg, egg yolks, and granulated sugar until well blended. Whisk in the flour, 1 tablespoon at a

time, and then continue whisking the mixture until it is thick and pale yellow, about 5 minutes. Slowly pour the hot milk into the egg mixture while stirring constantly. Then pour the contents of the bowl into the saucepan, place over low heat, and heat gently, stirring constantly, until the mixture is thick enough to coat the back of a spoon, about 7 minutes. Remove from the heat and pour through a fine-mesh sieve into a bowl. Stir in the Sambuca. Let cool to room temperature, stirring from time to time to prevent a skin from forming.

6 To assemble, using a serrated knife, cut the cake into slices about 2-by-3 inches (5-by-7.5 cm) and ¼ inch (6 mm) thick. Line the bottom of four 1-cup (8–fl oz/250-ml) bowls, preferably clear glass, with some of the cake slices. Sprinkle the cake with some of the rum. Spread one-fourth of the custard (about ½ cup/4 fl oz/125 ml) over the cake slices. Top with another layer of cake slices, and sprinkle with 2 tablespoons of the *alchermes*. Spread one-third of the remaining custard over the top. Repeat to make 2 more layers of cake, liqueur, and custard, and then end with a cake layer. Cover and refrigerate for several hours, or preferably overnight, before serving.

7 In a bowl, using a balloon whisk, combine the cream and confectioners' sugar and beat until medium-stiff peaks form. Spoon the cream on top of each bowl and sprinkle with the chocolate.

Follow this dessert with a glass of aged rum or Sambuca.

TORTA DELLA NONNA

Grandmother's Tart

This deceptively simple dessert—a rich, creamy custard filling topped with pine nuts and lined with a rich pasta frolla, *or short pastry—has long been a fixture of the Roman trattoria menu. Delicate ivory* pinoli, *the seeds of the stone pine, native to the Mediterranean, are encased in hard, dark shells attached to the outside of the pine cones found in profusion in the* pineti *(pine woods) around the city. This recipe, which adds the finely grated zest of a whole lemon to the custard, is, like the* torta di ricotta *on page 170, inspired by the* dolci *of gifted* pasticciere *Enrico Licata at La Piazzetta.*

1 To make the pastry dough, in a bowl, combine the butter, confectioners' sugar, honey, vanilla, lemon zest, and salt. Using your fingers, quickly and lightly work the ingredients together just until mixed. Using a wooden spoon, quickly work in the egg yolks. In a small bowl, whisk together the flour and baking powder. Gradually stir the flour mixture into the butter mixture. As soon as the ingredients come together, pat into a rough mass. Cover the bowl with plastic wrap and refrigerate the dough for at least 2 hours or for up to 24 hours.

2 Have ready a 9-inch (23-cm) tart pan with a removable bottom. Work the dough briefly to form a smooth mass. On a lightly floured work surface, roll out the dough into a round about 11 inches (28 cm) in diameter and ¼ inch (6 mm) thick. If the dough becomes too soft, return it to the refrigerator to chill until firm. Drape the round over the rolling pin and carefully ease it into the pan, gently pressing it into the bottom and up the sides. Trim off any excess dough, using the scraps to patch any holes and build up the sides of the tart if needed. Cover with plastic wrap and refrigerate while you prepare the filling.

3 To make the filling, in a saucepan over medium-low heat, combine the milk and ⅔ cup (5 oz/ 150 g) of the granulated sugar and heat, stirring, until the sugar dissolves. Continue to heat until bubbles appear along the edges of the pan. Remove from the heat and let cool slightly. Meanwhile, in a bowl, whisk together the remaining ⅓ cup (3 oz/90 g) sugar and the flour. Whisk in the egg yolks until well blended. Slowly pour about ½ cup (4 fl oz/125 ml) of the hot milk into the egg mixture while stirring constantly. Pour the mixture into the saucepan. Place over low heat and cook, stirring constantly, until the mixture is thick enough to coat the back of a spoon, 5–10 minutes. Remove from the heat and pour through a fine-mesh sieve into a bowl. Stir in the vanilla extract and lemon zest. Let cool to room temperature, stirring occasionally to prevent a skin from forming. Alternatively, place plastic wrap directly on the surface and refrigerate until cool, at least 30 minutes or up to 24 hours.

4 Preheat the oven to 375°F (190°C). Pour the cooled filling into the pastry-lined pan and sprinkle the pine nuts evenly on top. Place the tart pan on a rimmed baking sheet and bake until the top is just set and the crust is golden brown, about 35 minutes. Transfer to a wire rack and let cool completely. Remove the pan sides and slide the tart onto a flat serving plate. Serve at room temperature.

Serve with an Italian dessert wine, such as Moscato Passito di Pantelleria from Sicily or Muffato della Sala from Umbria.

FOR THE PASTRY DOUGH

6 tablespoons (3 oz/90 g) unsalted butter, at room temperature, cut into 6 pieces

⅔ cup (2½ oz/75 g) confectioners' (icing) sugar, sifted

1 tablespoon honey

Dash of vanilla extract (essence)

½ teaspoon grated lemon zest

Pinch of salt

2 large egg yolks

1¾ cups (7 oz/220 g) cake (soft-wheat) flour, sifted

½ teaspoon baking powder

FOR THE FILLING

2 cups (16 fl oz/500 ml) whole milk

1 cup (8 oz/250 g) granulated sugar

6 tablespoons (2 oz/60 g) all-purpose (plain) flour

4 egg yolks

⅛ teaspoon vanilla extract (essence)

Grated zest of 1 lemon

¼ cup (1½ oz/45 g) pine nuts

Makes one 9–9½-inch (23–24-cm) cake, or 8 servings

FONDENTE AL CIOCCOLATO

Rich Chocolate Cakes

While hardly a Roman tradition, a rich, dense chocolate cake is found on many of the city's dessert menus, including that of Ristorante Agata e Romeo, the inspiration for this recipe. It makes a fine showcase for Italian chocolate, whose purity was the subject of a debate that split the European Union in 2003, with France and Italy fighting to defend their superior products. Although the final ruling legalized the use of 5 percent other vegetable fats (a practice previously banned in Italy), it also brought improved labeling, a boon to consumers. Amedei chocolate, from Tuscany, is a favorite of Roman gourmets.

FOR THE CRÈME ANGLAISE

1 cup (8 fl oz/250 ml) whole milk

1 vanilla bean, split lengthwise, or ⅛ teaspoon vanilla extract (essence)

3 large egg yolks

⅓ cup (3 oz/90 g) sugar

FOR THE CAKES

1 cup (8 fl oz/250 ml) heavy (double) cream

7 oz (220 g) bittersweet chocolate, preferably 70 percent cacao, cut into small pieces

2 large egg yolks

2 tablespoons sugar

2 tablespoons all-purpose (plain) flour, sifted

Unsweetened cocoa powder for dusting

Makes 4 servings

1 To make the crème anglaise, in a saucepan over medium heat, combine the milk and the vanilla bean, if using (if using extract, add it later), and heat until small bubbles appear along the edges of the pan. Remove from the heat and let cool slightly. Meanwhile, in a bowl, whisk together the egg yolks and sugar until thick and pale yellow, about 5 minutes. Slowly pour the hot milk into the egg mixture while stirring constantly. Then pour the contents of the bowl into the saucepan, place over low heat, and heat gently, stirring constantly, until the mixture is thick enough to coat the back of a spoon, about 5–10 minutes. Remove from the heat and remove and discard the vanilla bean, if used. Pour the sauce through a fine-mesh sieve into a bowl. Stir in the vanilla extract, if using. Let cool to room temperature, stirring occasionally to prevent a skin from forming. Alternatively, place plastic wrap directly on the surface and refrigerate until cool, for at least 30 minutes or for up to 24 hours.

2 Preheat the oven to 425°F (220°C). Generously butter four ¾-cup (6–fl oz/180-ml) molds or ramekins, dust with flour, and tap out the excess.

3 To make the cakes, combine the cream and chocolate in a heatproof bowl placed over (not touching) barely simmering water, and heat, stirring occasionally, until the chocolate melts and the mixture is smooth and uniform. Remove from the heat and set aside to cool slightly.

4 In a bowl, using a whisk or a handheld mixer on medium speed, beat together the egg yolks and sugar until thick and pale yellow, about 5 minutes. Pour in the chocolate mixture in a thin stream while whisking constantly. Gently whisk in the flour.

5 Divide the chocolate mixture evenly among the prepared molds. Arrange the molds on a rimmed baking sheet. Bake until the top of each cake is firm to the touch, about 10 minutes. The center of each cake will still be liquid. Transfer the cakes, still in their molds, to a wire rack and let cool for 5 minutes.

6 To serve, invert a dessert plate over each warm cake and, holding the plate and mold, invert them together, then lift off the mold. If the cakes stick, ease them out with the tip of a knife. Spoon some of the cooled crème anglaise in a pool alongside each cake. Using a fine-mesh sieve or a sifter, dust each cake with a little cocoa powder. Serve at once, and pass the remaining crème anglaise at the table.

Chocolate is a tough match, but for a local wine, try Rosathea, a Moscato rosa from Castel de Paolis.

PECORINO CON PERE E CONFETTURA DI FICHI

Pecorino Romano with Sliced Pears and Fig Jam

Aged cheeses with fresh fruit and interesting, usually sweet condiments, such as artisanal honeys and fruit preserves, are popular desserts in the city's best restaurants. In winter, pecorino romano might be matched with pears and an easy jam made from dried figs, while in summer, it might sit alongside fresh figs so ripe they're bursting their seams. Figs have grown in and around Rome since ancient times, and today the season is split between the larger fruits of early summer and the small fruits (settembrini) of late summer.

1 To make the jam, preheat the oven to 300°F (150°C). Spread the nuts in a single layer on a small baking sheet and toast, shaking the pan every 8 minutes or so, until the nuts darken and give off a pronounced aroma, 10–15 minutes. Pour onto a plate to cool. (There is no need to remove the skins.)

2 In a small saucepan over high heat, combine the figs and ½ cup (4 fl oz/125 ml) water and bring to a boil. Remove from the heat and let stand for 5 minutes.

3 Put the nuts in a food processor and pulse twice. Add the figs and their liquid, the brandy, the 2 tablespoons sugar, and the lemon zest and juice and pulse until the figs are coarsely chopped. Taste and adjust with more sugar if needed.

4 Using a short, sharp knife, stab the cheese wedge and break off a chunk. Your goal is to make 4 nice chunks this way. Divide them among individual plates.

5 If the pear skins are blemish free, there is no need to peel them. Halve 1 pear, core it, and then thinly slice a pear half lengthwise, keeping the slices together. Fan the slices on a plate next to the cheese. Repeat with the remaining half and then the remaining pear. Divide the jam evenly among the plates. Alternatively, place the cheese and cheese knife on a board, fan the pear halves on a serving plate, put the jam in a small bowl, and let guests help themselves.

Serve with a sweet late harvest Est! Est!! Est!!! or a Muffato della Sala from just across the border in Umbria.

FOR THE FIG JAM

2 tablespoons hazelnuts (filberts) or almonds

¼ lb (125 g) moist dried figs (about 5 figs), stems trimmed and each fig cut into 4 or 5 pieces

2 tablespoons brandy

2 tablespoons sugar, or to taste

Grated zest and juice of ½ lemon

6-oz (185-g) wedge *pecorino romano* cheese, aged at least 5 months

2 ripe pears such as Bosc or Anjou

Makes 4 servings

Sheep's Milk Cheeses

The official animal of Rome is the she-wolf that nurtured the city's founder, Romulus, and his twin, Remus, but perhaps a more appropriate symbol would be *la pecora,* "the sheep." The boys grew up to be shepherds, and sheep have been grazing in or around Rome—urban sprawl permitting—ever since, with the result that the most typical local cheeses, including *pecorino romano* and *ricotta romana,* are made from sheep's milk.

The DOP regulation (page 81) for *pecorino romano* restricts its production to a zone that includes all of Lazio and Sardinia and the Grosseto province in southern Tuscany. The cheese must be made from whole milk from sheep raised in the zone, curdled with lamb rennet. It is aged for five months for a table cheese and at least eight months for a grating cheese and is considered an essential addition to *trippa alla romana* (tripe) and many pastas.

Ricotta romana is made from heated whey mixed with whole sheep's milk and heated again. The solids are then packed into conical baskets to drain. Mild and creamy, ricotta is great when fried (sweetened or not), on pasta, or in desserts.

PIZZA DI VISCIOLE ALLA ROMANA

Sour Cherry Tart

Visciole are small, sour cherries that grow near Rome, and any Roman lucky enough to have a friend with a tree looks forward to the early summer harvest. Most visciole, *like their even sourer relative,* amarene, *go straight into the jam pot, and it is the fate of most jams to end up spread in a thick tart crust. The use of the word* pizza, *rather than* crostata, *for this traditional Roman tart illustrates how the term was once applied to many kinds of cakes, breads, and pies. If you are short on time, use any good-quality commercial preserves—about 1 cup (10 oz/315 g)—that contains pieces of fruit.*

FOR THE CHERRY JAM

1 lb (500 g) sour cherries, pitted

½ cup (4 oz/125 g) granulated sugar

Pinch of ground cinnamon

FOR THE PASTRY DOUGH

1 whole egg plus 2 egg yolks

¾ cup (6 oz/185 g) granulated sugar

Pinch of salt

½ cup (4 oz/125 g) plus 2 tablespoons unsalted butter, at room temperature, cut into 6 pieces

3 cups (12 oz/375 g) cake (soft-wheat) flour

FOR THE PASTRY CREAM

1 cup (8 fl oz/250 ml) whole milk

1 large lemon zest strip

1 vanilla bean, split lengthwise

3 egg yolks

¼ cup (2 oz/60 g) granulated sugar

2 tablespoons cornstarch (cornflour)

1 egg yolk, lightly beaten

Confectioners' (icing) sugar

Makes one 11-inch (28-cm) tart, or 6–8 servings

1 To make the cherry jam, in a heavy nonreactive pan over medium heat, combine the cherries, granulated sugar, and cinnamon. Bring to a simmer, stirring constantly to dissolve the sugar, and then cook, stirring frequently, until the cherries have fully softened and are wrinkled and the mixture has thickened, about 15 minutes. Remove from the heat and set aside. The jam will thicken further as it cools.

2 To make the pastry dough, in a bowl, using a wire whisk, beat together the whole egg and egg yolks, granulated sugar, and salt until well blended. Gradually whisk in the butter a piece at a time until all of it has been incorporated. Add the flour a little at a time, working it in quickly with your fingers until it is incorporated and the dough is smooth. Divide the dough into 2 pieces, one slightly larger than the other. Form each piece into a disk, wrap separately in plastic wrap, and refrigerate for at least 2 hours or for up to 24 hours.

3 To make the pastry cream, in a saucepan over medium heat, combine the milk, lemon zest strip, and the vanilla bean, and heat until small bubbles appear along the edges of the pan. Remove from the heat, let cool slightly, and then remove and discard the lemon zest and the vanilla bean. Meanwhile, in a bowl, whisk together the egg yolks, granulated sugar, and cornstarch until thick and pale yellow, about 5 minutes. Slowly pour the hot milk into the egg mixture while `stirring constantly. Then pour the contents of the bowl into the saucepan, place over low heat, and cook, stirring constantly, until the mixture is thick enough to coat a spoon, 5–10 minutes. Remove from the heat.

Place the plastic wrap directly on the surface of the pastry cream and refrigerate for at least 30 minutes or up to 24 hours.

4 Preheat the oven to 350°F (180°C). Butter an 11-inch (28-cm) pie pan or tart pan with a removable bottom, dust with flour, and tap out the excess. Remove the larger disk from the refrigerator and place in the prepared pan. Using your hands, pat it evenly over the bottom and about 1 inch (2.5 cm) up the sides of the pan. Patch as necessary to create a smooth surface.

5 Spread the cooled pastry cream over the dough. Then, using a tablespoon, evenly dot the pastry cream with the jam. Using the back of the spoon, gently spread the jam over the top, covering the custard completely in an even layer.

6 On a lightly floured work surface, roll out the remaining disk into an 11-inch (28-cm) round. Using a pastry wheel, cut the round into 10 strips each about ¾ inch (2 cm) wide. Lay 5 strips across the filling. Lay the remaining 5 strips perpendicular to the first strips to create a lattice pattern. Cut off and discard any excess dough.

7 Bake the tart until the crust is golden brown, 40–45 minutes. Transfer to a rack and let cool completely. Dust with confectioners' sugar and serve.

Brachetto d'Acqui, a sweet effervescent red from Piedmont, is the perfect match for cherries.

GLOSSARY

ABBACCHIO In Rome, this term refers to a milk-fed baby lamb, less than two months old, as well as to young lamb in general. In local dishes, such as *abbacchio alla cacciatora* (page 139), lamb is always cooked through. The Italian word for lamb is *agnello*.

AL DENTE Literally meaning "to the tooth," this Italian phrase refers to pasta or rice that has been cooked until tender but is still firm at the center, thus offering some resistance to the bite. Most Italian-manufactured dried pastas have fairly accurate time recommendations on the package, but in general package times can run long.

ANCHOVIES Blended in a sauce or draped over pizza, tiny *acciughe*, or *alici*, appear widely in Italian cooking. Whole anchovies layered with salt have the best flavor of the preserved products. To prepare salt-cured anchovies, rinse them gently under cold running water. If a less assertive flavor is desired, soak for 10 minutes before proceeding. Scrape the skin of each anchovy away with the tip of a knife and cut away the dorsal fin. Press the anchovy open, flattening it carefully from head to tail end. Lift away the backbone, then cut the anchovy into 2 fillets. Rinse again, then dry on paper towels and use as directed in the recipe. Oil-cured anchovies come as fillets and do not need to be rinsed before using.

ARTICHOKES Artichokes (*carciofi*) are the signature vegetable of Rome, where they liven up the table in winter and spring. The city's market vendors and able cooks have perfected a painstaking method of cutting the bulbs in a circular pattern so that only what is edible remains (page 106). The most important use of artichokes is for *carciofi alla giudia* (page 53) and *carciofi alla romana* (page 159), but they also pop up in frittatas, pastas, and dishes such as *vignarola* (page 94).

BALSAMIC VINEGAR *Aceto balsamico tradizionale*, or traditional balsamic vinegar, comes from the area around Reggio Emilia and Modena in Emilia-Romagna. It is made from cooked Trebbiano and Lambrusco grape must. To be considered DOP *(denominazione origine protetta)*, it must be aged for at least 12 years in a series of barrels constructed of a variety of aromatic woods. The final product is slightly thick and syrupy, with a sweet, mellow taste,

and is used sparingly as a condiment on finished dishes. It should never be cooked. Less expensive versions of balsamic vinegar of varying quality are widely available; they can be used in vinaigrettes, marinades, and a variety of other preparations.

BASIL A member of the mint family, this iconic Mediterranean herb adds a highly aromatic flavor to foods when it is used fresh. It is traditionally paired with tomatoes and is considered an essential ingredient in many classic Italian dishes.

BAY LEAF Strong and spicy, the whole glossy leaves of the bay laurel tree are indispensable in long-simmered savory preparations, especially *ragù*. European bay leaves have a milder, more pleasant taste than the California-grown variety. The leaves are almost always sold dried and should be removed from a dish before serving.

BELL PEPPERS Sweet-fleshed, bell-shaped members of the pepper family, bell peppers (*peperoni*) are also known as sweet peppers or capsicums. Green bell peppers are usually more sharply flavored than red ones, the latter being simply a sweeter and more mature stage of the former. Orange and yellow bell peppers are separate varieties. Peppers traveled to Italy after Columbus's voyages to America and were at first cultivated for decorative purposes only, their edibility regarded with suspicion.

BREAD CRUMBS Used to make crisp toppings for oven-baked dishes or to lend body to fillings and stuffing, bread crumbs should be made from a slightly stale coarse country loaf. To make dried bread crumbs, trim the loaf of its crusts and process in a food processor to form crumbs. Dry the crumbs on a baking sheet in a preheated 325°F (165°C) oven for about 15 minutes; let cool, process again until fine, and continue baking, stirring once or twice, until pale gold, about 15 minutes longer.

BRESAOLA This salt-cured, air-dried beef is considered a specialty of the Valtellina, an Alpine valley in Lombardy. It is usually served thinly sliced like prosciutto. It tastes less salty than prosciutto, however, and its texture is firmer. Often paired with arugula and shaved parmesan, it is served as both an *antipasto* and a light *secondo*.

BROCCOLI RABE Although it is a relative of turnip greens (*cime di rapa*), broccoli rabe differs slightly in appearance. At the ends of its leafy green stems are clusters of broccoli-like florets. Be sure to remove any of the tough stems and wilted leaves before cooking. If the skin on the lower part of the stalks is fibrous, peel it with a vegetable peeler. Sautéed with garlic and chile, brocci rabe makes a terrific side dish.

CAPERS The preserved, unopened flower buds of a wild shrub, *capperi* have a piquant flavor enjoyed throughout the Mediterranean. Capers packed in sea salt retain their intense floral flavor and firm texture, but brined capers are more commonly available. Those labeled "nonpareil" are smaller than the distinctly large capers sold in Italian markets. Rinse both salted and brined capers before using.

CHICKPEAS Also known as garbanzo beans and in Italy as *ceci*, these round beige beans have a rich, nutty flavor and a firm texture. They hold their shape well during cooking, and are often used in hearty soups. Dried chickpeas must be soaked before using. Chickpeas sold in cans or in jars are a good alternative to the dried.

CHILES In Italy, small hot red chiles are known as *peperoncini*. Roman cooks add the fiery whole peppers to everything from pasta sauce to sautéed vegetables, and remove them before serving. (For milder fire, remove the seeds before using.) *Peperoncini* are available in well-stocked supermarkets and Italian or other specialty markets. Any small, dried red pepper will work as a substitute; alternatively, substitute ½ teaspoon red pepper flakes for the *peperoncino*.

DEEP-FRYING When done properly, deep-frying will yield light, tender seafood and vegetables. Maintaining a consistent high temperature causes the water naturally present in foods to convert to steam, which forces out any oil that might otherwise seep into the mix. A deep-frying thermometer is recommended for regulating the temperature. Adding foods to the hot oil in small batches will prevent large drops in temperature and ensure that foods are evenly immersed in the oil. In Italy, extra-virgin olive oil is typically used for frying.

EGGPLANT In Italian kitchens, eggplants (aubergines), called *melanzane*, are grilled; rolled, stuffed with a filling, and baked; or used in pasta sauces. The most familiar variety is the globe eggplant, which is usually large, resembles a pear in shape, and has a thin, shiny skin that ranges from ivory to lavender to deep purple. Many markets also carry elongated Italian eggplants. They are smaller than globe eggplants and have deep purple skin.

FAVA BEANS Pale green fava (broad) beans resemble lima beans but have a slightly bitter flavor. In spring, when the beans are at their most tender, slip them from their large pods and serve them raw with pecorino cheese. If the beans are older or larger, quickly blanch them and then remove the light green shell (though this is not done in Rome). Fresh and dried fava beans are very different and should not be substituted for each other in recipes.

FENNEL This vegetable, native to the Mediterranean region, is valued for its green-white bulb, feathery fronds, and pungent seeds. Fennel is at its best in winter, when the bulb adds its crisp texture and faintly sweet licorice flavor to salads. In Italy, raw fennel (*finocchio*) is often paired with oranges or other citrus. The bulbs can also be grilled or baked with Parmesan cheese. To use, cut off the long hollow stems and any discolored areas from the bulb, saving the feathery fronds to snip with scissors or to use whole as a garnish.

FIGS The ancient Romans believed figs, or *fichi*, imported from Greece were superior to those grown on local trees. Italians today are happy with their own harvests, eating them with prosciutto between slices of *pizza bianca*, baking them into breads, or mixing them with nuts and honey for cookies. Figs seem to flourish everywhere in Italy. They are cultivated in gardens and also grow wild, pushing their way through crevices in stone walls and ancient parapets. Many varieties ripen twice a year. In Rome, the small, sweet green or black figs of early autumn are called *settembrini* (little Septembers).

FLOUR

ALL-PURPOSE Also known as plain flour, all-purpose flour is made from a mixture of soft and hard wheats. It is often used for making breads.

CAKE Low in protein and high in starch, cake flour is milled from soft wheat and contains cornstarch. It is very fine in texture and has undergone a bleaching process that increases its ability to hold water and sugar. Cakes made with cake flour are less likely to fall. Cake flour is similar to the standard flour used in Italy for both savory and sweet recipes.

SEMOLINA This somewhat coarse flour is milled from durum wheat, a variety that is particularly high in protein. The flour is almost always used in the manufacture of dried pastas. It is also used in some pizza doughs and breads.

GUANCIALE See page 101.

HAZELNUTS Also known as filberts, and called *nocciole* in Italian, these nuts grow in abundance in northern Lazio and find their way into everything from biscotti to gelato. Grape-sized hazelnuts have hard shells that come to a point like an acorn, cream-colored flesh, and a sweet, rich, buttery flavor. They usually are sold already shelled.

MARJORAM The delicate floral flavor of marjoram blends beautifully with the other ingredients in many Italian recipes, especially when partnered with tomatoes. It has a milder flavor than oregano, a close cousin. Marjoram is best when used fresh.

OLIVE OIL See page 81.

ONIONS

GREEN ONIONS Although often used interchangeably with spring onions, green and spring onions are actually slightly different. The former are slim all the way from their dark green leaves down to the light green and white root, while the latter's white root protrudes into a rounded shape. Only spring onions are found in Italy, but the white and light green parts of the green onion can be substituted.

RED Also called Bermuda onions or Italian onions, red onions are purplish and sweet.

SHALLOT A small member of the onion family that looks like a large clove of garlic covered with papery bronze or reddish skin. Shallots, called *scalogni* in Italian, have white flesh lightly streaked with purple and a crisp texture. Their flavor is subtler than that of an onion.

SWEET VARIETIES One variety of Italian onion that has recently gained popularity abroad is the red *cipolla di Tropea,* named for a seaside town in Calabria. Medium sized and shaped like a top, they are almost always eaten fresh rather than cooked.

Vidalia or Maui onions, which are in season in spring and early summer, can be substituted, as can Walla Walla, another crisp and sweet variety.

WHITE This variety is the most common in Italian markets, though yellow onions are also common. It is more pungent than the red onion, but milder and less sweet than the yellow.

OXTAIL Oxtail, called *coda di bue* in Italian, now comes from steer and not oxen. They are usually sold sliced crosswise into 2-inch (5-cm) portions. Like short ribs, they are experiencing a rediscovery of sorts, as more people come to appreciate them as a traditional comfort food. Long, slow cooking mellows the meat and releases the gelatin from the bones, making a savory braise or stew.

PANCETTA See page 101.

PARSLEY, FLAT-LEAF This variety of the popular Mediterranean herb, called *prezzemolo* in Italian, has a more complex, peppery flavor than the curly-leaf type, which is rarely seen in Italy.

PASTA See page 36.

PINE NUTS These long, slender nuts, the seeds of umbrella-shaped stone pines that grow throughout the Mediterranean, are high in oil and have a delicate flavor. Called *pinoli* in Rome and *pignoli* in some other parts of Italy, pine nuts are used in both savory and sweet recipes. The nuts are sprinkled on pasta or added to meat sauces, and are used with fresh basil and olive oil to make *pesto alla genovese*. They are also an ingredient in some tarts and cakes, such as *Torta della Nonna* (page 177).

PIZZA PEEL Cooks, especially professional bakers, place garnished pizzas on this wooden tool so they can be transferred to and from the oven safely and with ease. Peels measure 24 inches (60 cm) or more in diameter and have a thin edge and long handle. A rimless baking sheet can be used for the same purpose.

PIZZA STONE Also called a baking stone or baking tile, this square, rectangular, or round slab of unglazed stoneware creates the effect of a brick oven in a home oven. The stone should be preheated in the oven for at least 45 minutes or up to 1 hour before baking. The pizza or other bread is slid onto the hot stone using a pizza peel.

PROSCIUTTO Prosciutto is made from the hind thigh of a pig just under a year old, and is cured at length under special conditions. Delicately flavored *prosciutto di Parma,* from the Emila-Romagna region, comes from pigs fed, among other things, whey left over from the Parmigiano-Reggiano cheese-making process. *Prosciutto di San Daniele,* from Friuli in northeastern Italy, is pressed into a distinctive violin-like shape, while Parma *prosciutti* are rounder. Both have dense, red meat and creamy, white fat. *Prosciutto di montagna* is a more generic term used in Rome to describe a less expensive, saltier, and more rustic style of prosciutto.

PUNTARELLE See page 45.

RED PEPPER FLAKES Flakes and seeds of *peperoncini,* slender dried red chiles, are a popular kitchen seasoning and table condiment in central and southern Italy. Just a pinch adds heat to many dishes. The chiles may be bought already crushed or may be purchased whole and crushed in a heavy-duty plastic bag with a rolling pin. When sautéing with red pepper flakes, be careful not to let them burn. See also Chiles.

ROSEMARY Taking its name from the Latin for "dew of the sea," reflecting its relationship to oceanside climates, this herb is native to the Mediterranean and contributes a powerful but pleasantly aromatic flavor to lamb, veal, chicken, and a host of other foods. It is, without a doubt, the most popular herb in Roman cooking.

SAGE An ancient healing herb that takes its name from the Latin *salvus,* meaning "safe," this heady, slightly musty-tasting herb (called *salvia* in Italian) is usually used fresh in Italian dishes. It is an essential ingredient in the dish *Saltimbocca alla Romana* (page 127).

SALT COD *Baccalà,* salt cod, is a fixture on Friday menus throughout Rome, in keeping with *il venerdi di magro,* the Catholic church's tradition of meatless Friday, which has become as much a gastronomic as a religious observance. The prevalence of salt cod in Italy harks back to the time when lack of refrigeration or rapid transport made access to fresh fish in inland cities nearly impossible. In the fifteenth century, whalers off the coast of Newfoundland learned to preserve precious Atlantic cod (*merluzzo,* in Italian) by salting it. They cleaned and salted the cod aboard the fishing boats, then dried it on land.

SAMBUCA This anise-flavored Roman liqueur can be enjoyed as a shot in coffee for *caffè corretto,* an after-dinner drink, or as a flavoring in desserts such as *zuppa inglese.* It is sometimes offered *con le mosche* (with flies), with two coffee beans floating freely in the glass.

SPAGHETTI FORK A spaghetti fork is a handy instrument with a long handle and a round, concave head with stubby tines and a hole in the middle. It is perfect for stirring strand pasta or retrieving it from the water once it is cooked.

TOMATOES See page 151.

ZUCCHINI In general, small zucchini (courgettes) are preferred for their few seeds and full flavor, and are often sold with their flowers still attached as an indication of freshness. The versatile squashes are cut into chunks, strips, or rounds, and deep-fried, sautéed, steamed, stewed, marinated, stuffed, grilled, or baked.

INGREDIENT SOURCES

A.G. FERRARI FOODS
Olive oil, pasta, cured meats, pecorino and other cheeses.

(877) 878-2783

www.agferrari.com

DI BRUNO BROTHERS
Will ship fine olive oils, pastas, some sheep's milk cheeses, and coffee from Illy, Kimbo, and Lavazza.

(888) 332-4337

www.dibruno.com

DITALIA
Source for aged *pecorino romano,* balsamic vinegar, Kimbo coffee, and more.

(888) 260-2192

www.ditalia.com

GUSTIAMO
A fine source for Italian pasta, rice, sweets, and even some Sabine olive oils.

(718) 860-2949

www.gustiamo.com

MANGIBENE
A range of cured meats, including *bresaola,* plus artisanal pastas, cheeses, and chocolates.

+39 045 634 8757

www.mangibene.it

NASO E GOLA
Prosciutto di Parma, balsamic vinegar, Amadei chocolate, and more.

(650) 756-6826

www.nasoegola.com

PAOLINO'S GOURMET ITALIAN FOOD
Sells artisanal pasta, including Latini brand, as well as extra-virgin olive oils.

(860) 653-3537

www.gourmetitalianfood.com

INDEX

gnocchi with Gorgonzola and radicchio, 118

sliced, baked whole fish with, 128

Prosciutto

about, 101, 187

baked farfalle with mushrooms, peas, and, 117

veal scallops with sage and, 127

Puntarelle

about, 45

with anchovy dressing, 160

Q

Quinto quarto, 143

R

Radicchio, potato gnocchi with Gorgonzola and, 118

Ravioli, fish, with oven-roasted cherry tomato sauce, 114

Red pepper flakes, 187

Restaurants

decor of, 17–18

ethnic, 14

history of, 12

by neighborhood, 25–27

service at, 17

standard setting, 18

Rice croquettes, 73

Ricotta

about, 170

mousse, strawberries with, 169

romana, 181

tart, 170

Rigatoni

about, 41

with *guanciale* and onion, 101

Rosemary, 187

Rosso Lazio, 57

Rughetta selvatica, 45

S

Sage, 187

Salads

fennel, orange, and olive, 78

puntarelle with anchovy dressing, 160

red, of tomatoes, carrots, and red onions, 151

of Roman field greens, 156

seafood, 85

Salt cod

about, 187

with raisins and pine nuts in tomato sauce, 132

Sambuca, 187

Sauces

béchamel, 117

crème anglaise, 178

oven-roasted tomato, 114

Seafood. *See also individual seafood*

about, 85

salad, 85

Semolina, 186

Sfogliatelle, 63

Shallots, 186

Shrimp, winter squash soup with, 97

Soups

pasta and chickpea, 93

winter squash, with shrimp, 97

Spaghetti

about, 41

forks, 187

with clams in their shells, 110

with eggs, cured pork, and cheese, 98

Spinach *(spinaci)*, 45

Sponge cake with custard and liqueur, 174

Squash. *See also* Zucchini

blossoms, fried, with mozzarella and anchovies, 77

soup, winter, with shrimp, 97

Strawberries with ricotta mousse, 169

T

Tarts

grandmother's, 177

onion and herb, 86

ricotta, 170

sour cherry, 182

Tiella, 86

Tomatoes

about, 151

chicken with sweet peppers and, 144

fettuccine with meat sauce, 113

garlic-rubbed toast with basil and, 69

pasta and chickpea soup, 93

pasta shells with mozzarella, basil, and, 105

pizza with roasted peppers, anchovies, and, 121

"red salad" of carrots, red onions, and, 151

rice croquettes, 73

romano beans with, 163

sauce, oven-roasted, fish ravioli with, 114

sauce, salt cod with raisins and pine nuts in, 132

stewed oxtail with celery and, 143

stuffed zucchini, 140

Tonnarelli with pecorino and pepper, 109

Tortelloni

about, 40

making, 39

Tozzetti, 173

Trattorias, 17, 18. *See also* Restaurants

V

Veal scallops with prosciutto and sage, 127

Vegetables. *See also individual vegetables*

growing, 42

stewed spring, 94

Vinegar, balsamic, 185

Visciole, 182

W

Water, 97

Wine

bars, 17, 54

DOC, DOCG, and IGT designations for, 54

of Lazio, 54, 56–57

varieties of, 56–57

Z

Zucchini

about, 187

blossoms, fried, with mozzarella and anchovies, 77

slices, marinated, 74

stuffed, 140

Zuppa inglese, 174

ACKNOWLEDGMENTS

Maureen B. Fant would like to thank, in particular, Mina Botti, Iris Carulli, Charlotte Cox, and Fanny Farkas for their invaluable help. Marinella Ercoli, Judith Harris, Howard Isaacs, Armando Manni, Maria Persia, Francesco Retacchi, Gwen and Franco Romagnoli, Bonnie Shershow, and Susan Wolf also provided assistance. A number of restaurateurs and chefs of Rome unselfishly shared recipes and advice: Sebastiano Allegrini, Enrico Licata and Franco Bartolini, Agata Parisella and Romeo Caraccio, Eugenio De Santis, Dario and Iole Cappellanti, Elio and Francesco Mariani, and Angelo and Massimo Troiani. In a class by herself is Oretta Zanini De Vita, walking encyclopedia of Italian food history and generous friend. Finally, there is Francesco Filippi—Franco—whose companionship, intelligence, and appetite were priceless stimuli at every stage.

Weldon Owen and the photography team, including Jean-Blaise Hall and George Dolese, wish to thank Elisa Zucchiatti for her incredible help and guidance, and Maureen Fant for going out of her way to lend a hand in Rome. They would also like to extend their gratitude to the owners and workers of restaurants, bakeries, shops, and other culinary businesses in Rome who participated in this project: Patrizia Mattei and the others at Antico Arco, Vittorio Procaccia at Vini e Buffet, Susy Porcelli and family at Checco er Carettiere, Claudio Ceccarelli at Hostaria Giggetto, Luciano Flamini at Maccherone, and the people at Al Vino Al Vino and Pizzeria Gaudi. A big thank you to Elizabeth and the staff at C.U.C.I.N.A for suppling us with a beautiful selection of tablewares. Jean-Blaise Hall in particular would like to thank his assistant Sandra Mahut for her great spirits on this project, as well as Trattoria Frontoni, Ristorante Paris, Pierluigi Roscioli and family at Roscioli, Casa Bleve, Pasticceria Vitti, Ristorante Il Convivio, Gelateria Giolitti, Checchino dal 1887, Antica Caciara, Panella bakery, fresh pasta shops Pasta Al'Uovo and Grand Gourmet, Hosteria Romana, Pasticceria Valzani, gourmet food shop Castroni, E. Volpetti & Co., Drogheria Innocenzi, Pizzeria Ai Marmi, Ristorante Agata e Romeo, Enoteca Cavour 313, Il Gelato di San Crispino, Dar Filettaro a Santa Barbara, Bar S. Eustachio, Tazza d'Oro, Gelateria Bar Sisto, La Rotonda, Ristorante Al Presidente, La Bottega del Cioccolato, 'Gusto, Ristorante La Rosetta, Enoteca Al Parlamento, butcher Angelo Feroa, the Antico Forno bakery, La Campannina restaurant in Ostia, and Trattoria Bucci in Castel Gandolfo. The team would also like to thank Susan and Joseph Miller for their generous hospitality and assistance, as well as Spark restaurant in Los Angeles and Oliveto and Citron restaurants in Oakland, California.

Weldon Owen wishes to thank the following individuals for their kind assistance: Desne Ahlers, Cecilia Brunazzi, Ken DellaPenta, Judith Dunham, Arin Hailey, Joan Olson, Stephanie Rosenbaum, Sharon Silva, and Paolo Sortino.

PHOTO CREDITS

Jean-Blaise Hall: All photography, except for the following:
Paul Moore: Pages 56–57
©Gustavo Tomsich/CORBIS: Page 155

PHOTOGRAPHY LOCATIONS

The following locations have been given map references for the map on pages 28–29.

PAGE	LOCATION (MAP COORDINATES)
4	Trevi Fountain (I2)
8	Hostaria Da Giggetto (H4)
10	Trajan's Forum (I4)
19	(top) Piazza Navona (G3)
20	Mercato di Piazza Testaccio (H7)
23	Mercato di Piazza Testaccio (H7)
26	(top left) Volpetti shop in Testaccio (H7)
27	Piazza Navona (G3)
30	Panella (K4)
34	(top left) Da Giggetto (H4)
37	(top, bottom left and right) La Campannina (off map)
43	(top) Mercato di Piazza Testaccio (H7)
43	(bottom left) Campo de' Fiori (G3)
47	(top) 'Gusto (H2)
47	(bottom center) Pizzeria Da Ivo (G5)
47	(bottom right) Roscioli (G3)
51	(bottom left) The synagogue (sinagoga) (H4)
59	(bottom left) Roscioli (G3)
59	(bottom center and right) Panella (K4)
79	Mercato di Piazza Testaccio (H7)
88	La Campannina (off map)
82	Piazza di Spagna (I2)
87	View from Gianicolo (F4)
100	'Gusto (H2)
111	La Campannina (off map)
114	Campo de' Fiori (G3)
138	Piazza Navona (G3)
143	Ox sculpture on the mattatoio, Testaccio (H7)
144	Woman on balcony, Rocca di Papa (off map)
153	Mercato di Piazza Testaccio (H7)
156	Saint Peter's (F2)
161	Campo de' Fiori (G3)
176	Isola Tibertina (H4)

OXMOOR HOUSE INC.

Oxmoor House books are distributed by Sunset Books
80 Willow Road, Menlo Park, CA 94025
Telephone: 650-321-3600 Fax: 650-324-1532
Vice President/General Manager Rich Smeby
National Accounts Manager/Special Sales Brad Moses
Oxmoor House and Sunset Books are divisions of
Southern Progress Corporation

WILLIAMS-SONOMA, INC.

Founder & Vice-Chairman Chuck Williams

THE FOODS OF THE WORLD SERIES

Conceived and produced by Weldon Owen Inc.
814 Montgomery Street, San Francisco, CA 94133
Telephone: 415-291-0100 Fax: 415-291-8841

In Collaboration with Williams-Sonoma, Inc.
3250 Van Ness Avenue, San Francisco, CA 94109

A Weldon Owen Production
Copyright © 2005 Weldon Owen Inc.
and Williams-Sonoma, Inc.

First printed in 2005
10 9 8 7 6 5 4 3 2 1

ISBN 0-8487-3006-2

Printed by Tien Wah Press
Printed in Singapore

WELDON OWEN INC.

Chief Executive Officer John Owen
President and Chief Operating Officer Terry Newell
Vice President International Sales Stuart Laurence
Creative Director Gaye Allen
Publisher Hannah Rahill
Business Manager Richard Van Oosterhout

Series Editor Kim Goodfriend
Project Editor Emily Miller
Editorial Assistant Juli Vendzules

Art Director Nicky Collings
Designers Alison Fenton, Rachel Lopez

Production Director Chris Hemesath
Color Manager Teri Bell
Production and Shipping Coordinator Todd Rechner

Food Stylist George Dolese
Associate Food Stylist Elisabet der Nederlanden
Prop Stylists George Dolese and Maggie Ward
Photographer's Assistants Sandra Mahut,
Jeremy Michael Weiss, Brooke Buchanan
Map Illustrator Bart Wright

JACKET IMAGES

Front cover: Coliseum; Pizza with Roasted Peppers,
Tomatoes, and Anchovies, page 121. Back cover:
fresh artichokes; view of Saint Peter's basilica;
man cutting Pecorino Romano cheese. Front flap:
man with *maritozzi*. Back flap: coffee from
Sant'Eustachio.

A NOTE ON WEIGHTS AND MEASURES

All recipes include customary U.S. and metric
measurements. Metric conversions are based on
a standard developed for these books and have
been rounded off. Actual weights may vary.